AF308018

Marx
Joyce
Abbott
Hardy
Austen
Defoe
Melville
Machiavelli
Chesterton
Cooper
Emerson
Hugo
Grimm
Montaigne
Haggard
Eliot
Stoker
Christie
Molière
Carroll
Wilde
Maupassant
Byron
Schiller
Garnett
Einstein
Fitzgerald
Hawthorne
Smith
Kafka
Goethe
Engels
Cotton
Dostoyevsky
Hall
Baum
Kipling
Doyle
Willis
Henry
Nietzsche
Leslie
Dumas
Flaubert
Turgenev
Balzac
Stockton
Vatsyayana
Crane
Burroughs
Verne
Curtis
Tocqueville
Gogol
Vinci
Homer
Whitman
Busch
Widger
Tolstoy
Darwin
Thoreau
Potter
Twain
Scott
Freud
Zola
Plato
Harte
Kant
Jowett
Lawrence
Dickens
Stevenson
Burton
Andersen
Hesse
London
Descartes
Cervantes
Voltaire
Poe
Aristotle
Wells
Cooke
Hale
James
Hastings
Bunner
Shakespeare
Irving
Richter
Chambers
da
Doré
Dante
Chekhov
Shaw
Benedict
Alcott
Swift
Wodehouse
Pushkin
Newton

 tredition®

tredition was established in 2006 by Sandra Latusseck and Soenke Schulz. Based in Hamburg, Germany, tredition offers publishing solutions to authors and publishing houses, combined with world-wide distribution of printed and digital book content. tredition is uniquely positioned to enable authors and publishing houses to create books on their own terms and without conventional manufacturing risks.

For more information please visit: www.tredition.com

TREDITION CLASSICS

This book is part of the TREDITION CLASSICS series. The creators of this series are united by passion for literature and driven by the intention of making all public domain books available in printed format again - worldwide. Most TREDITION CLASSICS titles have been out of print and off the bookstore shelves for decades. At tredition we believe that a great book never goes out of style and that its value is eternal. Several mostly non-profit literature projects provide content to tredition. To support their good work, tredition donates a portion of the proceeds from each sold copy. As a reader of a TREDITION CLASSICS book, you support our mission to save many of the amazing works of world literature from oblivion. See all available books at www.tredition.com.

Project Gutenberg

The content for this book has been graciously provided by Project Gutenberg. Project Gutenberg is a non-profit organization founded by Michael Hart in 1971 at the University of Illinois. The mission of Project Gutenberg is simple: To encourage the creation and distribution of eBooks. Project Gutenberg is the first and largest collection of public domain eBooks.

Correggio A Collection Of Fifteen Pictures And A Portrait Of The Painter With Introduction And Interpretation

Estelle M. (Estelle May) Hurll

Imprint

This book is part of TREDITION CLASSICS

Author: Estelle M. (Estelle May) Hurll
Cover design: Buchgut, Berlin – Germany

Publisher: tredition GmbH, Hamburg - Germany
ISBN: 978-3-8472-2889-9

www.tredition.com
www.tredition.de

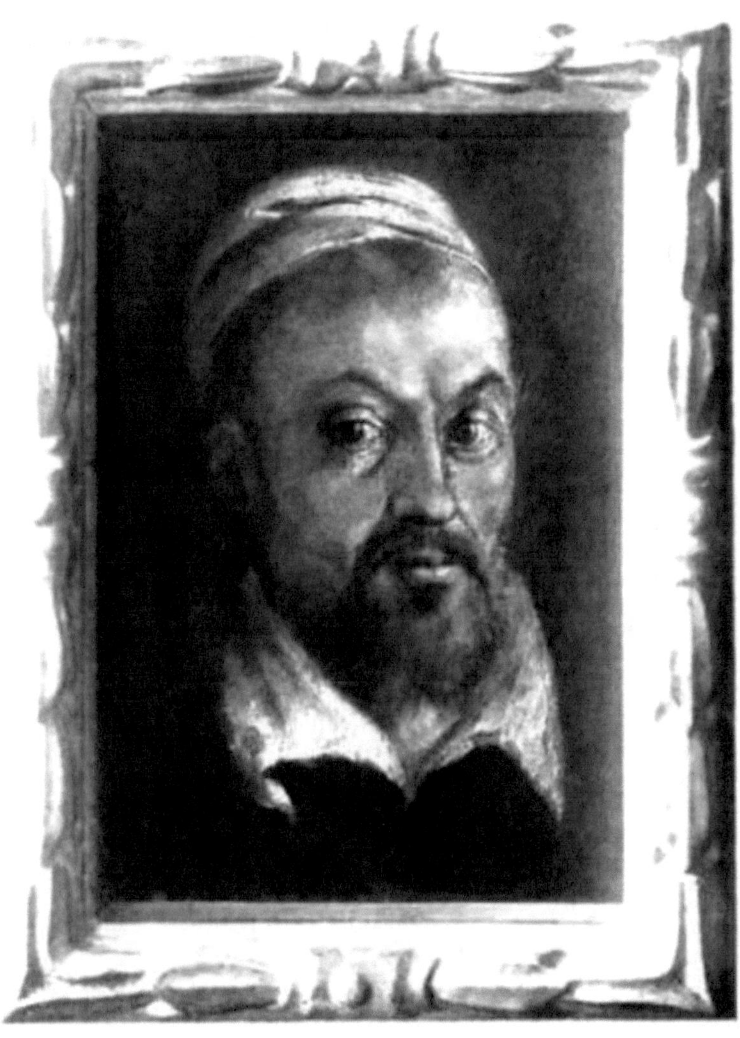

A SUPPOSED PORTRAIT OF CORREGGIO
Parma Gallery

Masterpieces of Art

CORREGGIO

A COLLECTION OF FIFTEEN PICTURES

AND A SUPPOSED PORTRAIT OF THE

PAINTER, WITH INTRODUCTION

AND INTERPRETATION

BY

ESTELLE M. HURLL

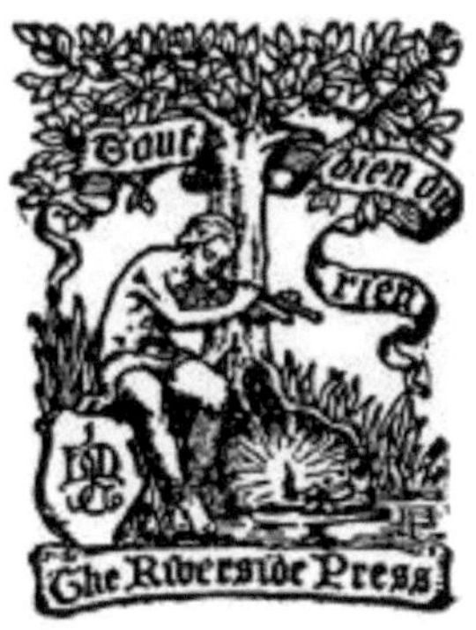

PREFACE

To the general public the works of Correggio are much less familiar than those of other Italian painters. Parma lies outside the route of the ordinary tourist, and the treasures of its gallery and churches are still unsuspected by many. It is hoped that this little collection of pictures may arouse a new interest in the great Emilian. The selections are about equally divided between the frescoes of Parma and the easel paintings scattered through the various European galleries.

ESTELLE M. HURLL.

New Bedford, Mass.

December, 1901.

CONTENTS AND LIST OF PICTURES

[vii]

INTRODUCTION

I. ON CORREGGIO'S CHARACTER AS AN ARTIST.

The art of Correggio was very justly summed up by his first biographer, Vasari. After pointing out that in the matter of drawing and composition the artist would scarcely have won a reputation, the writer goes on to say: "To Correggio belongs the great praise of having attained the highest point of perfection in coloring, whether his works were executed in oil or in fresco." In another place he writes, "No artist has handled the colors more effectually than himself, nor has any painted with a more charming manner or given a more perfect relief to his figures." Color and chiaroscuro were undoubtedly, as Vasari indicates, the two features of his art in which Correggio achieved his highest triumphs, and if some others had equalled or even surpassed him in the first point, none before him had ever solved so completely the problems of light and shadow.

Not only did he understand how to throw the separate figures of the picture into relief, giving them actual bodily existence, but he mastered as well the disposition of light and shade in the whole composition. To quote Burckhardt, "In Correggio first, chiaroscuro becomes essential to the general expression of a pictorially combined whole; the stream of lights and reflections gives exactly the right expression to the special moment in nature."

The quality of Correggio's artistic temperament was [viii] essentially joyous. [1] The beings of his creation delight in life and movement; their faces are wreathed with perpetual smiles. Hence childhood and youth were the painter's favorite subjects. The subtleties of character study did not interest him; and for this reason he failed in representing old age. He was perhaps at his best among that race of sprites which his own imagination invented, creatures without a sense of responsibility, glad merely to be alive.

[1] Tradition says that the temperament of the man himself was exactly the reverse of that of the artist, being timid and melancholy.

This temperament explains why the artist contented himself with so little variety in his types. We need not wonder at the monotony of the Madonna's face. She is happy, and this is all the painter required of her psychically. He took no thought even to make her beautiful: the tribute he offered her was the technical excellence of his art,—the exquisite color with which he painted flesh and drapery, the modulations of light playing over cheek and neck. With hair and hands he took especial pains, and these features often redeem otherwise unattractive figures.

In his predilection for happy subjects Correggio reminds us of Raphael. The two men shrank equally from the painful. But where the Umbrian's ideal of happiness was tranquil and serene, Correggio's was exuberant and ecstatic. Raphael indeed was almost Greek in his sense of repose, while Correggio had a passion for motion. "He divines, knows and paints the finest movements of nervous life," says Burckhardt.

Even when he sought to portray a figure in stable equilibrium, he unwittingly gave it a wavering pose; witness the insecurity of Joseph in the Madonna della Scodella, and of St. Jerome in the Madonna bearing his name. Usually he preferred some momentary attitude caught in [ix] the midst of action. In this characteristic the painter was allied to Michelangelo, the keynote of whose art is action.

It is a curious fact that two artists of such opposed natures—the one so light-hearted, the other burdened with the prophet's spirit—should have so much in common in their decorative methods. Both understood the decorative value of the nude, and found their supreme delight in bodily motion. In a common zeal for exploiting the manifold possibilities of the human figure, the two fell into similar errors of exaggeration. In point of design Correggio cannot be compared with Michelangelo. He was utterly incapable of the sweeping lines characteristic of the great Florentine. He seldom achieved any success in the flow of drapery, and often his disposition of folds is very clumsy.

It is interesting to fancy what Correggio's art might have been had he been free to choose his own subjects. Limited, as he was, in his most important commissions, to the well-worn cycle of ecclesiastical themes, he could not work out all the possibilities of his genius. Nevertheless, he infused into the old themes an altogether new spirit, the spirit of his own individuality. It is a spirit which we call distinctly modern, yet it is as old as paganism.

Among the works of the old Italian masters, Correggio's art is so anomalous that it has inevitably called forth detractors. What to his admirers is mere childlike sweetness is condemned as "sentimentality," innocent playfulness as "frivolity," exuberance of vitality as "sensuality." Certainly there is nothing didactic in his art. "Space and light and motion were what Antonio Allegri of Correggio most longed to express," [2] and to these aims he subordinated all motives of spiritual significance. One of his severest critics (Burckhardt) has conceded that "he [x] is the first to represent entirely and completely the reality of genuine nature." He, then, who is a lover of genuine nature in her most subtle beauties of "space and light and motion," cannot fail to delight in Correggio.

[2] E. H. Blashfield in Italian Cities.

II. ON BOOKS OF REFERENCE.

The first biographer of Correggio was Vasari, in whose "Lives of the Painters, Sculptors, and Architects" is included a brief account of this painter. The student should read this work in the last edition annotated by E. H. and E. W. Blashfield and A. A. Hopkins. Passing over the studies of the intervening critics, Julius Meyer's biography may be mentioned next, as an authoritative work, practically alone in the field for some twenty-five years. This was translated from the German by M. C. Heaton, and published in London in 1876. Finally, the recent biography by Signor Corrado Ricci (translated from the Italian by Florence Simmonds, and published in 1896) may be considered almost definitive. It is issued in a single large volume, profusely illustrated. The author is the director of the galleries of Parma, and has had every opportunity for the study of Correggio's works and the examination of documents bearing upon his life.

General handbooks of Italian art giving sketches of Correggio's life and work are Kugler's "Handbook of the Italian Schools," revised by A. H. Layard, and Mrs. Jameson's "Early Italian Painters," revised by Estelle M. Hurll.

For a critical estimate of the art of Correggio a chapter in Burckhardt's "Cicerone" is interesting reading, but the book is out of print and available only in large libraries. In "Italian Cities," by E. H. and E. W. Blashfield, a delightful chapter on Parma describes Correggio's works and analyzes his art methods. Morelli's "Italian Painters" [xi] contains in various places some exceedingly important contributions to the criticism of Correggio's works. The author's repudiation of the authenticity of the Reading Magdalen of the Dresden Gallery has been accepted by all subsequent writers.

Comments on Correggio are found in Symonds's volume on "The Fine Arts" in the series "The Renaissance in Italy," and are also scattered through the pages of Ruskin's "Modern Painters" and Hazlitt's "Essays on the Fine Arts." The volume on Correggio in the series "Great Masters in Painting and Sculpture" is valuable chiefly for a complete list of Correggio's works. The text is based on Ricci. [3]

[3] As this book goes to press Bernard Berenson's "The Study and Criticism of Italian Art" makes its appearance. A portion of it is devoted to the study of Correggio.

III. HISTORICAL DIRECTORY OF THE PICTURES OF THIS COLLECTION.

Portrait frontispiece. From a photograph of an alleged portrait of Correggio in the Parma Gallery.

1. *The Holy Night.(La Notte.)* (Detail.) Painted at the order of Alberto Pratoneri for the altar of his chapel in the church of S. Prospero, Reggio. Agreement signed October 10, 1522. Stolen from the church May, 1640, and taken to Modena. Now in the Dresden Gallery. Size of whole picture: 8 ft. 5 in. by 6 ft. 2 in.

2. *St. Catherine Reading.* Conjectural date, 1526-1528. In Hampton Court Gallery. Size: 2 ft. 1 in. by 1 ft. 8 in.

3. *The Marriage of St. Catherine.* Date, according to Meyer, 1517-1519; according to Ricci, after 1522. Painted for the Grillenzoni family of Modena. After several transfers it came into the possession of Cardinal Mazarin, from whose heirs it was acquired for Louis XIV.'s [xii] collection and hence became a permanent possession of the Louvre Gallery, Paris. Size: 3 ft. 5-1/3 in. by 3 ft. 4 in.

4 and 5. *Ceiling Decoration,* and *Diana,* in the Sala del Pergolata, Convent of S. Paolo, Parma. Frescoes painted in 1518.

6, 7, and 8. *St. John the Evangelist, St. John and St. Augustine, St. Mark and St. Jerome.* Frescoes in the church of S. Giovanni Evangelista, Parma. Painted 1520-1525.

9. *The Rest on the Return from Egypt.* (*La Madonna della Scodella.*) According to Pungileoni painted 1527-1528; according to Ricci, 1529-1530. The frame containing the picture is supposed to have been designed by Correggio himself. It bears the date 1530, when the picture was placed in the church of S. Sepolcro, Parma. Taken as French booty in 1796, but returned to Parma in 1816. Now in the Parma Gallery. Size: 7 ft. 3 in. by 4 ft. 6 in.

10. *Ecce Homo.* According to Ricci, painted during a visit to Correggio, 1521-1522; probably first belonged to the Counts Prati, of Parma. In the seventeenth century there were three pictures of the subject in Italy claiming to be the original. This picture was formerly in the Colonna family; now in the National Gallery, London. Size: 3 ft. 2-1/2 in. by 2 ft. 7-1/2 in.

11 and 12. *Apostles and Genii,* and *St. John the Baptist.* Frescoes in the Cathedral of Parma. Painted 1524-1530.

13. *Christ appearing to Mary Magdalene in the Garden.* (*Noli me tangere.*) Assigned by Ricci to 1524-1526. Described by Vasari as the property of the Ercolani family of Bologna. Passing from one owner to another, it was finally presented to Philip IV. of Spain, and is now in the Prado Gallery, Madrid. Size: 1 ft. 3-1/3 in. by 1 ft. 6-1/2 in. [xiii]

14. *The Madonna of St. Jerome.* (*Il Giorno.*) Ordered in 1523 by Donna Briseide Colla, for the church of S. Antonio, Parma. Painted 1527-1528, according to Ricci. After the destruction of this church it was placed in the Cathedral for safety. Seized by Napoleon in 1796. Finally returned to Parma, and now in the Parma Gallery. Size: 4 ft. 8 in. by 6 ft. 10 in.

15. *Cupid sharpening his Arrow.* (Detail of *Danaë.*) Ordered (1530-1533) by Federigo II., Duke of Mantua, as a gift for the Emperor Charles V. After passing through many hands it came in 1823 into the possession of the Borghese family, and is now in the Borghese Gallery, Rome. Size of whole picture, 5 ft. 4 in. by 6 ft. 5 in.

IV. OUTLINE TABLE OF THE PRINCIPAL EVENTS IN CORREGGIO'S LIFE.

Compiled from Ricci's Correggio, *to which the references to pages apply.*

1494. Antonio Allegri born at Correggio.

1511-1513. Probably in Mantua (p. 69).

1515. Madonna of St. Francis (p. 94).

1518. In Parma executing the frescoes of San Paolo, April-December (p. 152).

1520. Invitation to Parma from the Benedictines (p. 153). Marriage with Girolama Merlini (p. 185).

1520-1525. At work on frescoes of S. Giovanni Evangelista, Parma, with interruptions as noted below (pp. 189-195).

July, 1521-Spring, 1522. In Correggio (pp. 194, 195), and probable execution of the Ecce Homo, Christ in Garden, and Noli me tangere (p. 226).

1521. Birth of son Pomponio, September 3 (p. 185). [xiv]

1522. Visit to Reggio and commission for the Nativity (La Notte) October (pp. 195, 294). Commission for frescoes of Parma Cathedral, November (p. 250).

1523. Visit in Correggio (p. 195). Order for Madonna of St. Jerome (p. 278).

1524. Last payment for frescoes of S. Giovanni (p. 190). Birth of daughter Francesca Letizia, December 6 (p. 185).

1524-1530. Work on frescoes of the Parma Cathedral, interrupted by visits to Correggio, as noted below (p. 273).

1525. Visits to Correggio in February and August (p. 274). Madonna of St. Sebastian painted for Confraternity of St. Sebastian at Modena (p. 275).

1526. Birth of daughter Caterina Lucrezia (p. 185).

1527. Visits in Correggio (p. 274).

Circa 1528. Birth of daughter Anna Geria (p. 185).

1528. Visit in Correggio in summer (p. 274).

1529. Death of wife (p. 185).

1530-1534. In Correggio (p. 307). Mythological pictures for Federigo Gonzaga (p. 311).

1534. Death of Allegri, March 5 (p. 326).

V. LIST OF CONTEMPORARY ITALIAN PAINTERS.

- Vincenzo Catena, Venetian, 1470-1532.
- Michelangelo, Florentine, 1475-1564.
- Lorenzo Lotto, Venetian, circa 1476-1555.
- Bazzi (Il Sodoma), Sienese, 1477-1549.
- Giorgione, Venetian, 1477-1510.
- Titian, Venetian, 1477-1576.
- Palma Vecchio, Venetian, 1480-1528.
- Lotto, Venetian, 1480-1558. [xv]
- Raphael, Umbrian, 1483-1520.
- Pordenone, Venetian, 1484-1539.
- Bagnacavallo, Bolognese, 1484-1542.
- Gaudenzio Ferrari, Milanese, 1484-1549.
- Sebastian del Piombo, Venetian, 1485-1547.
- Andrea del Sarto, Florentine, 1486-1531.
- Bonifazio Veneziano, Venetian, circa 1490-1540.
- Cima da Conegliano, Venetian, 1493-1517.
- Pontormo, Florentine, 1493-1558.
- Moretto, Brescian, 1500-1547.
- Bronzino, Florentine, 1502-1572.
- Basaiti, Venetian, first record, 1503-last record, 1520.

[1]

I

THE HOLY NIGHT (LA NOTTE) (Detail)

In the northern part of Italy is the little town of Correggio, which
gave its name to the painter whose works we are to study. His real
name was Antonio Allegri, but in the sixteenth century a man
would often be called by a nickname referring to some peculiarity,
or to his birthplace. When Allegri went to Parma he was known as
Antonio da Correggio, that is, Antonio from Correggio, and the
name was then shortened to Correggio.

A large part of Correggio's work was mural decoration, painted
on the surface of the plastered wall. Besides such frescoes he painted many separate pictures, mostly of sacred subjects to be hung
over the altars of churches. The choice of subjects was much more
limited in his day than now, and, with the exception of a few mythological paintings, all Correggio's themes were religious. The subject most often called for was that of the Madonna and Child. Madonna is the word, meaning literally My Lady, used by the Italians
when speaking of Mary, the mother of Jesus. The Madonna and
Child is then a picture of the mother Mary holding the Christ-child.
[2]

Our illustration is from such a picture called "La Notte," the Italian for The Night. The night meant by the title is that on which Jesus
was born in Bethlehem of Judæa. It was at a time known in history
as the Augustan Age, when Rome was the great world-power.
Judæa was only an obscure province of the vast Roman Empire, but
here was the origin of the influence which was to shape later history. The coming of Jesus brought a new force into the world.

The story of his infancy has been made familiar by the four Evangelists. He was born in surroundings which, in Roman eyes, were fit
only for slaves. Mary and Joseph had come up from their own home
to Bethlehem to pay the taxes exacted at Rome. The town was full of
people on the same errand, and "there was no room for them in the
inn." So it came about that the new-born babe was wrapped in
swaddling clothes and laid in a manger used for feeding cattle.

While he lay in this strange cradle his birth was made known by a
vision of angels to some shepherds on the neighboring hillsides. At
once they betook themselves joyfully to Bethlehem, the first to do
honor to the new-born king. These homely visitors are gathered

about the manger in Correggio's picture. The dark night is without, but a dazzling white light shines from the Holy Child.

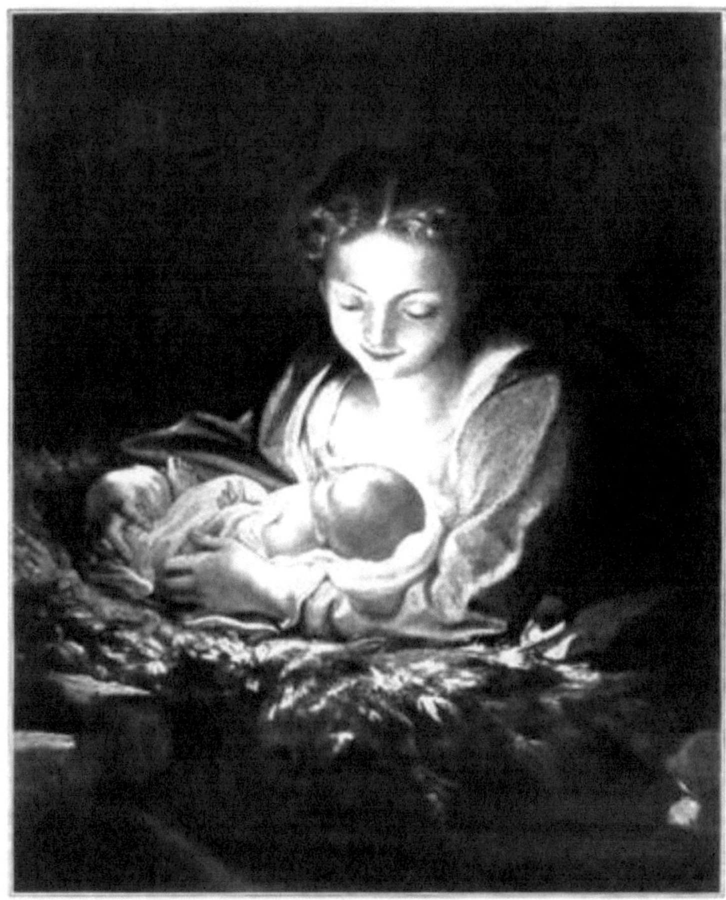

THE HOLY NIGHT (DETAIL)
Dresden Gallery

Please click on the image for a larger image.

Please click here for a modern color image

Our illustration shows only the centre of the picture, where the mother leans over her babe. The little form lies on a bundle of hay, completely encircled by her arms. The bend of her elbow makes [5] a soft pillow for his head; her hands hold him fast in the snug nest. With brooding tenderness she regards the sleeping child.

A white cloth is wrapped loosely about the baby's body — the swaddling band, which, when tightly drawn, is to hold the figure straight. The fingers of one hand peep out from the folds, and one little foot is free. For the rest we see only the downy top of the baby's head and one plump shoulder. The little figure glows lite an incandescent body, and the mother's face is lighted as if she were bending over a fire. It is a girlish face, for we are told that Mary was a very young mother. The cares of life have not yet touched the smooth brow. In her happiness she smiles fondly upon her new treasure.

We have no authentic description of Mary, the mother of Jesus, but it is pleasant to try to picture her in imagination. As her character was a model of womanliness, it is natural to believe her face correspondingly beautiful. The old masters spent their lives in seeking an ideal worthy of the subject, and each one conceived her according to his own standards of beauty. Correggio's chief care was for the hair and hands, which he painted, as we see here, with exquisite skill. He was usually less interested in the other features, and the Madonna of our picture is exceptionally lovely among his works of this kind.

The picture of La Notte illustrates very strikingly an artistic quality for which Correggio is famous. This is *chiaroscuro*, or the art of light and shadow, — the art by which the objects and figures of a [6] picture are made to seem enveloped in light and air, as in the actual world. The contrast between the bright light in the centre and the surrounding darkness gives vivid reality to the figures. There is also a symbolic meaning in the lighting of the picture. Christ is "the light of the world;" hence his form is the source of illumination.

Our picture was originally called by the simple title of The Nativity. Then the Italians, struck by the power with which the effect of midnight was produced, called it "La Notte," The Night. When it came to a German gallery the Germans called it "Die Heilige Nacht," The Holy Night. An old German Christmas carol interprets it so perfectly that it seems as if the author must have known the picture. These are the verses:—

> "Silent night! Holy Night!
> All is calm, all is bright
> Round you, virgin mother and child;
> Holy infant, so tender and mild,
> Sleep in heavenly peace,
> Sleep in heavenly peace.
>
> "Silent Night! Holy Night!
> Shepherds quake at the sight.
> Glories stream from Heaven afar,
> Heavenly hosts sing alleluia.
> Christ the Saviour is born!
> Christ the Saviour is born!
>
> "Silent Night! Holy Night!
> Son of God, love's pure light
> Radiant beams from Thy holy face
> With the dawn of redeeming grace,
> Jesus, Lord, at thy birth,
> Jesus, Lord, at thy birth."

[7]

II

ST. CATHERINE READING

The story of St. Catherine is very quaintly told in the old legend. [4] She was the daughter of "a noble and prudent king," named Costus, "who reigned in Cyprus at the beginning of the third century," and "had to his wife a queen like to himself in virtuous governance." Though good people according to their light, they were pagans and worshippers of idols.

[4] The life of St. Catherine is related in the *Golden Legend*. See Caxton's translation in the *Temple Classics*, volume vii., page 1. Mrs. Jameson also gives an outline of the story in *Sacred and Legendary Art*, p. 459.

Even in her babyhood the child Catherine was "so fair of visage" that all the people rejoiced at her beauty. At seven years of age she was sent to school, where "she drank plenteously of the well of wisdom." Her father was so delighted with her precocity that he had built a tower containing divers chambers where she might pursue her studies. Seven masters were engaged to teach her, the best and "wisest in conning" that could be found. So rapid was their pupil's progress that she soon outstripped them in knowledge, and from being her masters they became her disciples.

When the princess was fourteen, her father died, [8] leaving her heir to his kingdom. A parliament was convened, and the young queen was crowned with great solemnity. Then arose a committee of lords and commons, petitioning her to allow them to seek some noble knight or prince to marry her and defend the kingdom. Now Catherine had secretly resolved not to marry, but she answered with a wisdom not learned altogether from books. She agreed to marry if they would bring her a bridegroom possessing certain qualifications which she knew were impossible to fulfil. This silenced the counsellors, and she continued to reign alone.

In the course of time Queen Catherine became a Christian and devoted herself to works of religion and charity. Under her teaching many of her people were converted to the faith. It was a happy kingdom until the Emperor Maxentius chanced to visit the royal city. He was a tyrant who persecuted Christians. Upon his arrival he ordered public sacrifices to idols, and all who would not join in the heathen ceremony were slain. Then Catherine went boldly to meet the emperor and set forth to him the errors of paganism. Though confounded by her eloquence he was not to be convinced by the words of a mere woman. Accordingly he summoned from divers provinces fifty masters "which surmounted all mortal men in worldly wisdom." They were to hold a discussion with the queen and put her to confusion. For all their arguments, however, Catherine had an answer. So complete was her victory that the entire company declared themselves Christians. The angry emperor [11] caused them all to be burned and cast Catherine into prison.

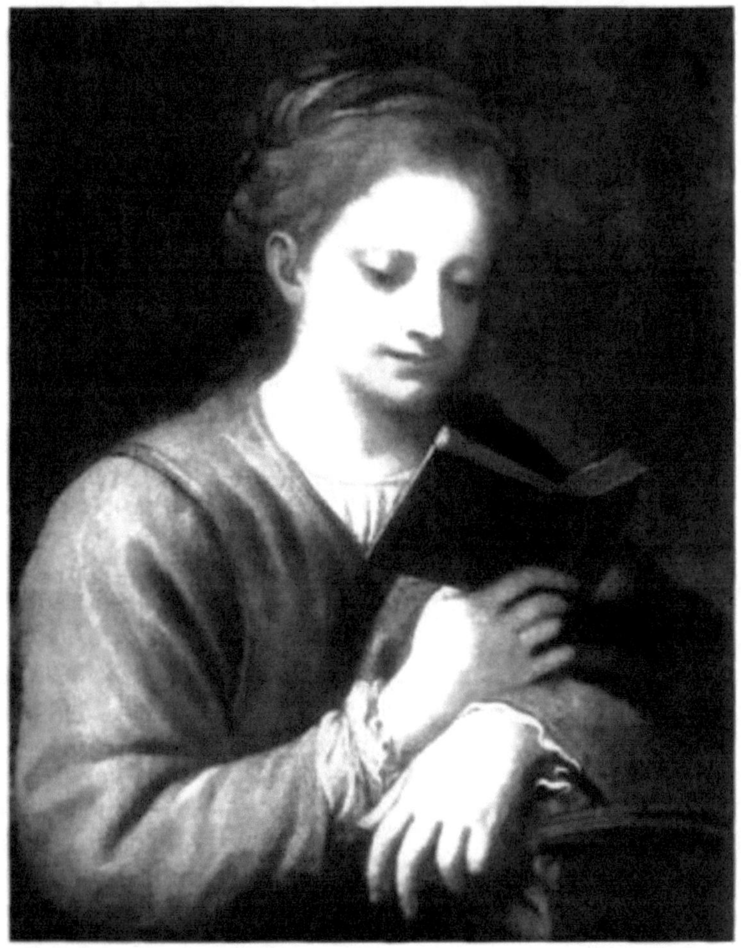

ST. CATHERINE READING
Hampton Court Gallery, London

Please click on the image for a larger image.

Even here she continued her good works, converting the empress and a prince who came to visit her. A new torment was then devised for her. Iron wheels were made, bound with sharp razors, and she was placed between these while they were turned in opposite directions. "And anon as this blessed virgin was set in this torment, the angel of the Lord brake the wheels by so great force that it slew four thousand paynims." Maxentius then commanded that she should be beheaded, and St. Catherine went cheerfully to her death.

Other virgin martyrs may have been as good and as beautiful as St. Catherine, but none were so wise. We know her in our picture by the book she holds. Eager to acquire all the treasures of knowledge, she fixes her eyes on the page, absorbed in her occupation. Already she has read more than half the thick volume, smiling with quiet enjoyment as she reads. There is little in the face to suggest the scholar or the bookworm. Were this a modern picture, we should fancy it a young lady reading her favorite poet. As it is, however, we must believe that the book is some work by Plato or another of the ancient writers whom St. Catherine could quote so readily. We need not wonder that she does not knit her brow over any difficult passages. What might be hard for another to grasp is perfectly clear to her understanding.

The beautiful hair coiled over her head is the only [12] coronet the princess wears. There is no sign of her royalty, and we may infer that the picture represents her in those early days of girlhood before the cares of government were laid on the young shoulders. As we study the position of the figure we see that the left arm rests on the rim of a wheel, making a support for the hand holding the book. The wheel is the emblem most frequently associated with St. Catherine, as the reminder of the tortures inflicted by Maxentius. The palm branch caught in the fingers of the left hand is the symbol used alike for all the martyrs. The reference is to that passage in the book of Revelation which describes the saints standing before the throne "with palms in their hands." [5]

[5] Revelation vii. 9.

It is pleasant to believe that Correggio took unusual pains with this picture of St. Catherine. The story of the lovely young princess seems to have appealed to his imagination, and he has conceived an ideal figure for her character. The exquisite oval of the face, the delicate features, and the beautiful hair make this one of the most attractive faces in his works.

The light falls over the right shoulder, casting one side of the face in shadow. The modulations of light on the chin and neck, and the gradation in the shadow cast by the book on the hand, show Correggio's mastery of chiaroscuro.

[13]

III

THE MARRIAGE OF ST. CATHERINE

At the time of her coronation, St. Catherine knew nothing of the Christian faith, but she had set for herself an ideal of life she was determined to carry out. It was her firm resolve not to marry. Her counsellors argued that, as she was endowed with certain qualities above all creatures, she ought to marry and transmit these gifts to posterity. The attributes they enumerated were, first, that she came of the most noble blood in the world; second, that she was the richest living heiress; third, that she was the wisest, and, fourth, the most beautiful of all human beings.

The young queen replied that she would marry only one who possessed corresponding qualities. "He must be," she said, "so noble that all men shall do him worship," so rich that "he pass all others in riches," so full of beauty "that angels have joy to behold him;" and finally, he must be absolutely pure in character, "so meek that he can gladly forgive all offences." "If ye can find such an one," she declared, "I will be his wife with all mine heart, if he will vouchsafe to have me."

Of course all agreed that there never was and never would be a man such as she described, and [14] the matter was at an end. To Catherine, however, there came a strange conviction that her ideal was not an impossible one. All her mind and heart were filled with the image of the perfect husband she had conceived. She continually mused how she might find him.

While she thought on these things, an old hermit came to her one day saying that he had had a vision, and had been sent with the message that her chosen bridegroom awaited her. Catherine at once arose and followed the hermit into the desert. Here it was revealed to her that the perfect man she had dreamed of was Jesus, the Christ, and to this heavenly bridegroom she was united in mystic marriage. Returning to her palace she wore a marriage ring, as the perpetual token of this spiritual union.

The story explains the subject of our picture. The Christ-child, seated on his mother's knee, is about to place a ring on St. Catherine's finger, while St. Sebastian looks on as a wedding guest. The infant bridegroom performs his part with delight. He holds the precious circlet between the thumb and forefinger of his right hand, and with his left singles out St. Catherine's ring finger. The bride's hand rests on the mother's open palm, held beneath as a support.

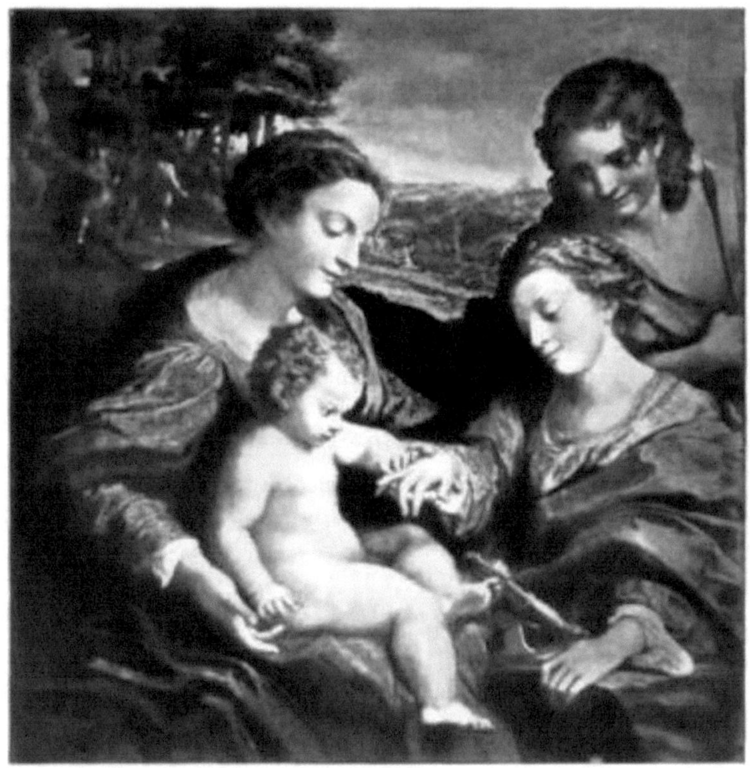

THE MARRIAGE OF ST. CATHERINE
The Louvre, Paris

Please click on the image for a larger image.

Please click here for a modern color image

All are watching the child's motions intently; the mother with
quiet pleasure, St. Sebastian with boyish curiosity, and St. Catherine
herself with sweet seriousness. Any comparison of the scene with a
human marriage is set aside by the fact that the [17] bridegroom is
an infant. The ceremony is of purely spiritual significance, a true
sacrament. St. Catherine's expression and manner are full of humility, as in a religious service.

The Christ-child is a robust little fellow whose chief beauty is his
curls. He has the large head which usually shows an active temper-

ament, and we fancy that he is somewhat masterful in his ways. We shall see the same boy again in the picture called The Madonna of St. Jerome.

The mother, too, has a face which soon becomes familiar to the student of Correggio's works. The eyes are full, the nose is rather prominent, the mouth large and smiling, and the chin small. Even St. Catherine is of the same type, except that her face is cast in a smaller and more delicate mould. Her hair is arranged precisely like that of the Madonna, the braids bound about the head, preserving the pretty round contour. Both women wear dresses cut with round low necks, showing their full throats. St. Catherine's left hand rests upon a wheel with spiked rim, which, as we have seen, is her usual emblem. Another emblem is the sword, whose hilt projects from behind the wheel. This was the instrument of her execution.

Special prominence is given in the picture to three sets of hands. The skill with which they are painted is noted by critics as one of the many artistic merits of the work. One of Browning's poems [6] describes an artist's meditations while trying to draw a hand. [18] His failure teaches him to realize that he must study the

> "Flesh and bone and nerve that make
> The poorest coarsest human hand
> An object worthy to be scanned
> A whole life long for their sole sake."

Such must have been Correggio's study to enable him to produce the beautiful hands we see here.

[6] *Beside the Drawing Board.*

St. Sebastian is a figure not to be overlooked. We may find his like among the genii of the Parma Cathedral, which we are to study. He is a joyous being to whom it is good merely to be alive. The elfin locks falling about his face make him look like some creature of the woods. We are reminded most of the faun of the Greek mythology. The arrows in his hand suggest some sylvan sport, but in reality they are the emblem of his martyrdom. According to tradition the young saint was bound by his enemies to a tree, and shot with arrows.

Behind the group stretches a bit of open country, and if we look closely we can discern here two groups of small figures. One represents the martyrdom of St. Sebastian, and the other, the execution of St. Catherine. We may suppose that such gruesome subjects were not the choice of the painter. It is probable that they were dictated by his patrons, and in obeying orders he made the figures as inconspicuous as possible.

[19]

IV

CEILING DECORATION IN THE SALA DEL PERGOLATO

(HALL OF THE VINE TRELLIS)

(S. Paolo, Parma)

In the time of Correggio the convent of S. Paolo (St. Paul) in Parma was in charge of the abbess Giovanna da Piacenza, who had succeeded an aunt in this office in 1507. She was a woman of liberal opinions, who did not let the duties of her position entirely absorb her. She still retained some social connections and was a patroness of art and culture. The daughter of a nobleman, she was a person of consequence, whose private apartments were such as a princess might have. Already a well known painter of the day had decorated one of her rooms when she heard of the rising artist Correggio. Probably advised by her relative the Cavaliere Scipione Montino, she commissioned the young painter to fresco a second room.

The decorative scheme he designed is very beautiful and elaborate. The square ceiling is completely covered with a simulated trellis, embowered in foliage and flowers, and pierced by oval windows through which children are seen at play. A circle in the centre contains the family arms of the abbess, a shield on which three crescent moons are set diag [20] onally. From this centre, as from the hub of a wheel, a series of gilded ribs radiate towards the sides, cutting the whole space into triangular sections whose surfaces are slightly hollowed. The oval windows of the trellis open in these sections, one in each triangle, and sixteen in all. Above every window hangs a bunch of fruit, seemingly suspended from the centre by ribbons fancifully braided about the ribs. The outer edge of the design, where the ceiling joins the walls, is finished by a series of sixteen lunettes or semicircles running around the square, one in each section. The frieze around the side walls simulates a narrow scarf caught up in festoons between ornamented capitals formed of rams' heads. The remaining decoration of the room is on the cap of the chimney, and represents the goddess Diana setting forth for the chase.

This picture furnishes the subject of the children's games in the lattice bower. The little sprites are attendants of the goddess, playing in a mimic hunt. Two or three may be seen through every window, busy and happy in their innocent sport. One is the delighted possessor of a quiver of arrows, from which he draws a shaft. Others play with the hounds, pulling them hither and thither at their will. A group of five find the hunting-horn an amusing plaything, and good-humoredly strive together over the treasure.

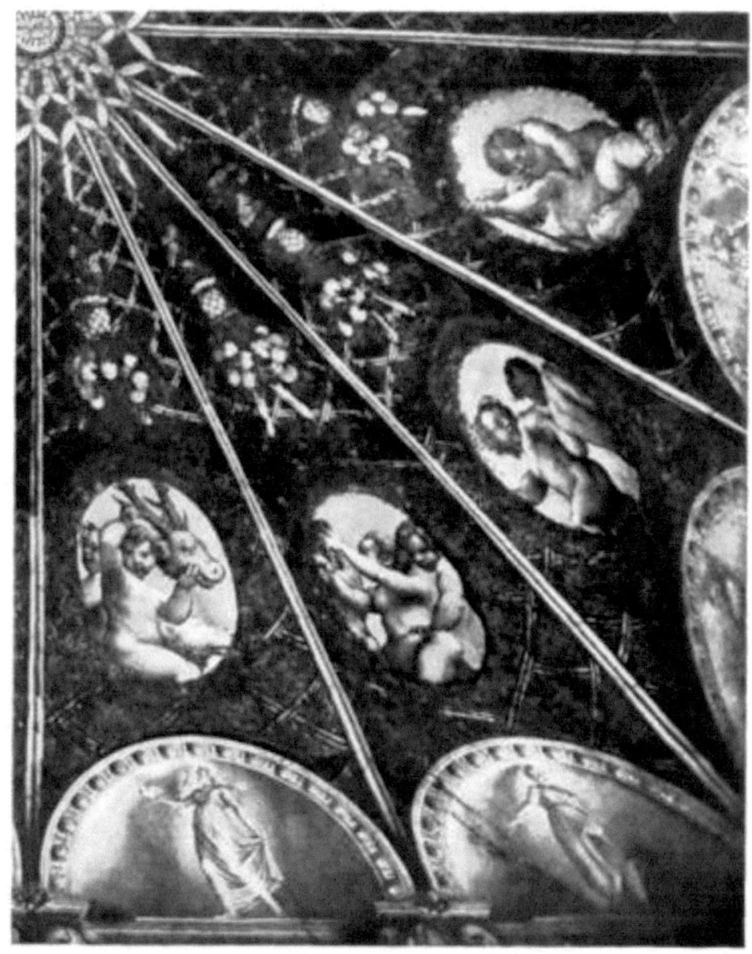

CEILING DECORATION IN THE SALA DEL PERGOLATO
Convent of S. Paolo, Parma

Please click on the image for a larger image.

Our illustration shows a quarter section of the ceiling, from which we can in imagination reconstruct [23] the whole diagram. [7] Let us see what the children are doing in this corner of the lattice. At the window directly in front of us a little fellow proudly exhibits a stag's head as a trophy of the chase. Just behind his shoulder a merry companion, peeps out, and lower down, on the other side, appears the head of an animal like a doe. In the next window is a boy with a wreath of flowers with which he and a companion apparently mean to crown the head of the stag. The third boy of the group has for the moment lost interest in the play, his attention being attracted by something going on outside. Now comes a boy passing by the next window, who hastens to join the party we have just seen. His playfellow wants to go the other way, and tries to detain him. "Come," he says, seizing him by the arm, "there's no fun over there. See what I have found."

[7] A quarter section, mathematically exact, is of course, square in shape. In our illustration the lower part of two lunettes is cut off.

We are somewhat at a loss to know just what mischief the baby in the next window has been plotting. He grasps with both hands a tall staff, which may be a hunting-spear, or perhaps a pole with which he hopes to reach the fruit. In some way he has managed to get both feet through the window, and is now in a precarious position, half in and half out. His companion tries to draw him in; but whether he is alarmed at the danger, or is himself eager to get the pole, we cannot tell.

The lunettes of the ceiling are painted in gray, [24] framed in borders of sea-shells. They are made to simulate niches containing sculptured figures with some allegorical or mythological meaning. In our illustration we see first the figure of Chastity, holding in her right hand the dove, which is the emblem of innocence. The dress is the long, plain tunic seen in Greek sculpture, and the thin stuff of which it is made flows in graceful lines about the form. We are reminded of Milton's lines in "Comus:" —

> "So dear to Heav'n is saintly Chastity,
> That when a soul is found sincerely so,
> A thousand liveried angels lacky her,
> Driving far off each thing of sin and guilt,
> And in clear dream and solemn vision,
> Tell her of things that no gross ear can hear."

The next figure is similar in character and meaning. It is Virginity, holding in her right hand the lily, which is the symbol of purity. The other two figures, of which we see only the upper portion, are Fortune, with a cornucopia, and the helmeted Athena, with spear and torch.

At the death of the abbess Giovanna in 1574, the convent of S. Paolo entered upon a period of severe ecclesiastical discipline. For more than two centuries it was impossible for outsiders to gain admittance, and the "Sala del Pergolato" was a sealed treasure. Finally, in 1794, the Academy of Parma gained permission to examine Correggio's paintings. After the suppression of the convent the room was thrown open to the public, and the building is now used for a school.

[25]

V

DIANA

In classic mythology, Diana, the Greek Artemis, was the goddess of the moon, twin sister of the sun-god Apollo. As the rays of moonlight seem to pierce the air like arrows, Diana, like Apollo, was said to carry a quiver of darts; the slender arc of the crescent moon was her bow. Thence it was natural to consider her fond of hunting, and she became the special patroness of the chase and other sylvan sports. Her favorite haunts were groves and lakes, and she blessed the increase of field and meadow. She was mistress of the brute creation, and showed special favor to the bear, the boar, the dog, the goat, and the hind. The poet Wordsworth has described how the ancient huntsman regarded the goddess:—

> "The nightly hunter lifting up his eyes
> Towards the crescent moon, with grateful heart
> Called on the lovely wanderer who bestowed
> That timely light to share his joyous sport;
> And hence a beaming goddess with her nymphs
> Across the lawn and through the darksome grove
> (Not unaccompanied with tuneful notes
> By echo multiplied from rock or cave)

Swept in the storm of chase, as moon and stars
Glance rapidly along the clouded heaven
When winds are blowing." [8]

[8] In *The Excursion.* [26]

There were other pleasant beliefs about Diana such as might be connected with the thought of the moon. As the moonlight cheers the traveller on his way and enters the chamber of the sick and lonely, so Diana was said to watch with the sick and help the unfortunate. The pale, white light of the moon is a natural symbol of purity, hence Diana was a maiden goddess above all allurements of love. Her worship was conducted with splendid rites in various ancient cities. The temple built in her honor at Ephesus was famous as one of the seven wonders of the world.

The ancients naturally liked to fancy the goddess very beautiful. The Greek poet Anacreon called her "the goddess of the sun bright hair." The English Keats, who delighted in the old Greek myths, has also described the charms of "the haunter chaste of river sides, and woods and heathy waste." [9] She had "pearl round ears, white neck, orbed brow, blush tinted cheeks," and "a paradise of lips and eyes."

[9] In *Endymion.* See also Lowell's *Endymion* for a description of Diana.

In our picture the moon goddess is mounting her car for the nightly course across the sky. [10] Though she seems to be but just springing to her place, with bending knee, she is already speeding on her way.

[10] As Apollo drives the sun chariot across the sky by day. Compare Guido Reni's Aurora.

"How tremulous-dazzlingly the wheels sweep
Around their axle."

Her quiver, well filled with the bow and arrows, [29] hangs at her back, held by the strap bound over her breast. [11] The crescent moon gleams above her brow. The vehicle is the small two-wheeled chariot used among the Romans, scarcely larger than a chair. Only the hind legs of the steeds may be seen, but we fancy them to be two white does.

[11] It seems odd that with this full quiver the subject should be called by some "Diana's Return from the Chase."

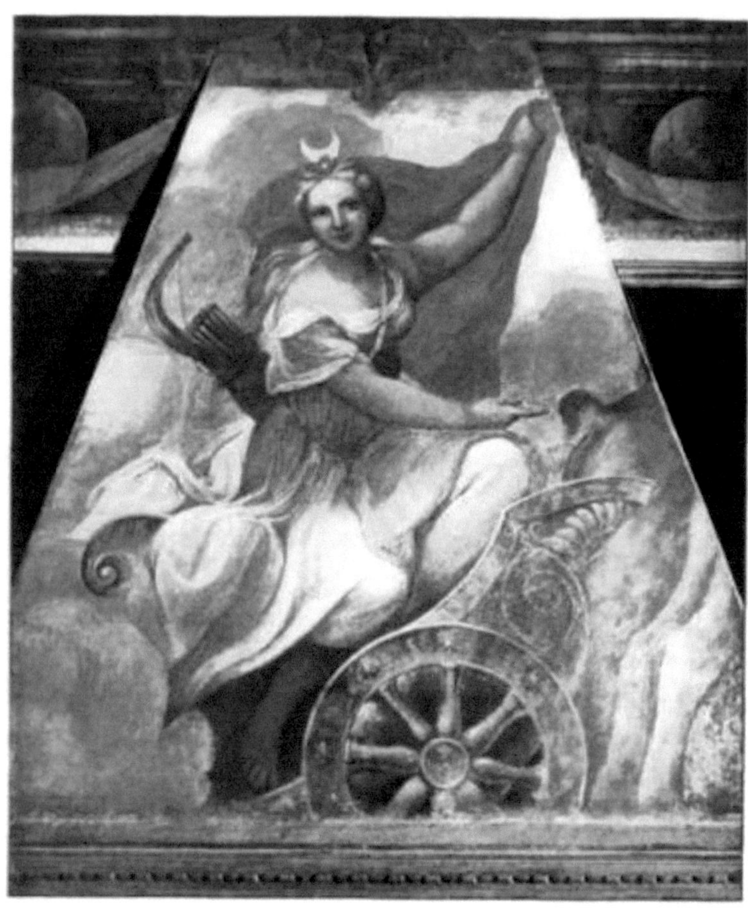

DIANA
Convent of S. Paolo, Parma

Please click on the image for a larger image.

Please click here for a modern color image

The huntress turns her face earthward, lifting a fluttering veil high in her left hand. It is as if the face of the moon had been hidden behind a cloud which the goddess suddenly draws aside and shows "her fulgent head uncovered, dazzling the beholder's sight." It is with a bright, cheerful countenance that she beams upon her worshippers. A sense of courage and exhilaration is expressed in her spirited bearing. With her right hand she points forward, as if calling us to join in the sport. In the swiftness of her motion her unbound hair and filmy garments blow out behind her.

She is a country-bred maiden, with plump neck and round arms, and her chief charm is her buoyant vitality. Her open face, with eyes set rather far apart, is the index of her nature. Her free life in the woods has developed a well poised womanhood. Fear is unknown to her; pain and disease come not near her. Rejoicing in immortal youth and strength, she speeds nightly through the sky, the messenger of light and comfort.

As we have seen in the preceding chapter, the picture of Diana is painted in fresco on the chimney [30] cap, or hood, over the great fireplace in the Hall of the Vine Trellis. We may well believe that the decoration went far towards furnishing the stately apartment. Underneath runs the Latin inscription, "*Ignem gladio ne fodias,*" stir not the fire with the sword.

It will be remembered that the arms of the abbess, for whom the room was decorated, bore the device of the crescent moon. This fact may have suggested to Correggio, or his patrons, the subject of the moon goddess. Diana, as a virgin divinity, was an especially appropriate choice for the apartment of a nun.

The legends of Greek mythology were at that time very popular among people of culture, having been recently brought to notice in the revival of classic learning. In Italy they furnished themes for the painter; in England, for the poet. The English Ben Jonson, living a half a century later than Correggio, [12] but representing in a certain measure the same love of classic allusion, wrote a "Hymn to Diana," which might have been inspired by this picture. The first stanza may be quoted for its interpretation: —

> "Queen and huntress, chaste and fair,
> Now the sun is laid to sleep,
> Seated in thy silver chair,
> State in wonted manner keep.
> Hesperus entreats thy light,
> Goddess excellently bright."

[12] That is, from 1573 to 1637.

[31]

VI

ST. JOHN THE EVANGELIST

It seemed understood among the twelve disciples of Jesus that John was the one of their number especially beloved by the Master. He and his brother, James, were the sons of the fisherman Zebedee, and all three men earned their living in their fishing-boats on the sea of Galilee. It was while they were busy with their nets that Jesus one day called the two brothers to be fishers of men. "And they straightway left their nets and followed him." [13]

[13] St. Matthew, chapter iv., verse 20.

Under the teachings of Jesus, John grew in knowledge of spiritual things. He was one of the three accompanying their Master to the Mount of Transfiguration, where they witnessed a sacred scene withheld from the others. His nature was affectionate and poetic, and he was a deep thinker. Often when the meaning of Jesus' words was beyond his hearers, John treasured the sayings in his memory. On the evening when Jesus sat at table with his disciples for the last time, John was near him, leaning on his Master's breast. When, on the next day, Jesus hung upon the cross, it was John to whom he commended his mother as to a son. "And from that hour that disciple took her unto his own home." [32]

In the years that followed, John pursued his Christian service with the zeal of an ardent nature. He remained awhile in Judæa and, in company with Peter, added many converts to the faith. He then carried the work into Asia Minor, where he founded seven churches. Not only was he a preacher and organizer, but a voluminous writer as well. The fourth Gospel is believed to be his work, in which he records many words and deeds of Jesus overlooked by the other Evangelists. He was also the writer of the three Epistles which bear his name. Finally, he is supposed to be the author of the book of Revelation, in which he described his visions during his exile in the isle of Patmos. According to tradition, he lived to a great age, and died at Ephesus in Asia Minor.

The love with which Christians cherish the memory of St. John is seen in the number of churches bearing his name. One such is that in Parma which was newly built at the time when Correggio was winning his first laurels. The most important portions of the interior decorations were executed by our painter.

Before considering the frescoes of the cupola, the visitor to the church likes to pause before the lunette over the door of the left transept. The subject is St. John, seated with his writing materials on his lap. There is a pile of books behind him and a volume beside him. At his feet stands the symbolic eagle pluming his wing.

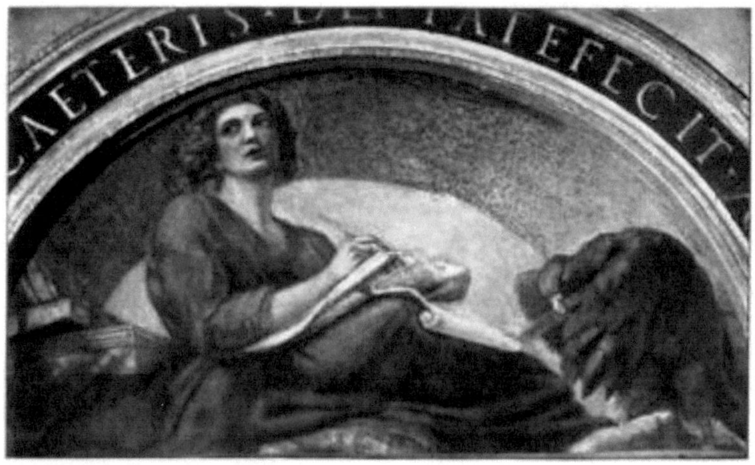

ST. JOHN THE EVANGELIST
Church of S. Giovanni Evangelista, Parma

Please click on the image for a larger image.

The emblems of the Evangelists are drawn from [35] Ezekiel's vision of the "four living creatures," whose faces were those of a man, a lion, an ox, and an eagle. Applied respectively to the writers of the four Gospels, each emblem suggests some characteristic trait. The eagle is especially appropriate to St. John. As the bird soars into the upper regions of the sky and looks directly at the sun, so St. John's inspiration raised him into the highest realms of thought, where he seemed to gaze directly upon the divine glory. It is for this that he is called St. John, "the divine." As the Latin inscription over the lunette reads, "More deeply than the others he disclosed the mysteries of God." [14]

[14] "Altius cœteris Dei patefecit arcana."

In our picture the Evangelist lifts his eyes heavenward as if beholding a vision. His lips are parted, and he has the rapt expression of one absorbed in meditation. His right hand still holds the pen as he pauses for inspiration.

In trying to do honor to the beloved disciple, the painters have always represented him as the most beautiful of the twelve. As the most Christ-like in character, he is made to resemble the typical figure of Christ. So in this fresco by Correggio, he is a beautiful youth, with the curling hair, the oval face and the regular features we associate with the person of Jesus. Though the beardless face is so refined, there is nothing weak or effeminate about it. The whole figure is indeed very manly. The head is well set on a full throat and the shoulders are broad. Rising to his feet St. John would be a [36] tall, athletic young man, capable of lending a strong hand at his father's fishing-nets. The union of strength and refinement makes the picture one of the most attractive ideals of St. John ever painted.

The keynote of St. John's Gospel is the love of God; his ardent nature never wearied of the theme; the wonder in his lifted face shows him still intent upon the mystery. Were we to seek some characteristic utterance which should appropriately interpret his thoughts, it might well be the words of Jesus to Nicodemus, "God so loved the world that he gave his only begotten son, that whosoever believeth in him should not perish, but have everlasting life." [15]

[15] St. John, chapter iii., verse 16.

[37]

VII

ST. JOHN AND ST. AUGUSTINE

The church of S. Giovanni Evangelista (St. John the Evangelist), in Parma, is built with a dome-shaped cupola which Correggio filled with a fresco decoration. The subject is drawn from the life of the apostle whose name is given to the church: it is the vision of St. John on the isle of Patmos. Looking up into the dome, one seems to be looking directly into the open sky, upon the figure of Christ ascending into heaven. The apostles sit in a circle on the clouds, and beneath them the aged St. John kneels on the mountain top, gazing upwards upon the vision. The heavenly spaces are alive with angels, for, as Browning writes: —

> "Correggio loves to mass, in rifts
> Of heaven, his angel faces, orb on orb."

The little creatures are sporting among the clouds and, in the poet's phrase, "waiting to see some wonder momently grow out."

Where the dome rests upon the four arches which support it, are four triangular corner-pieces called pendentives, which also belong to Correggio's decorative plan. They are devoted respectively to the figures of the four Evangelists, each one accompanied by one of the four Fathers of the Church. The [38] Christian Fathers were the men whose writings and teachings shaped the doctrines of the faith in the early centuries of our era. They interpreted for the people the meaning of the Scriptures and the Gospels.

The pendentive of our illustration contains St. John with St. Augustine. The two sit side by side, engaged in a discussion over the book which they hold together. St. John is young and beautiful, as the painters always represent him, except in the subject of the vision of Patmos. The face is perhaps less strong and the expression less exalted than in the lunette we have studied. There is a boyish eagerness in his manner. The symbolic eagle is beside him, peeping out from the folds of the drapery. St. Augustine is a handsome old man with finely cut features. To understand how well the figure fits his character, we must know something of his life. [16]

[16] The life of St. Augustine, also called St. Austin, is related in the *Golden Legend*. See Caxton's translation in the *Temple Classics*, vol. 5, page 44. Mrs. Jameson gives a condensed account of the life in *Sacred and Legendary Art*, p. 303.

He was born in Numidia near the middle of the fourth century, and showed in his boyhood brilliant powers of mind. Without the help of any teacher he read and mastered all the books necessary to an education in the liberal arts. His mother, Monica, was a devout Christian, and sought to lead her son to a godly life. For a long time her efforts seemed in vain. Augustine would make no profession of the Christian faith, but rather indulged in youthful [41] dissipations. His best quality was his love of study. He became a teacher of rhetoric, and pursued his vocation in one city and another, always dissatisfied with his life. At length, in his thirtieth year, he came to Milan, where he fell under the influence of Bishop Ambrose. Then followed a mighty struggle in his soul, and in the end he yielded himself joyfully as a disciple of Christ. On the occasion of his baptism was composed the hymn called the "Te Deum" which is still used in churches.

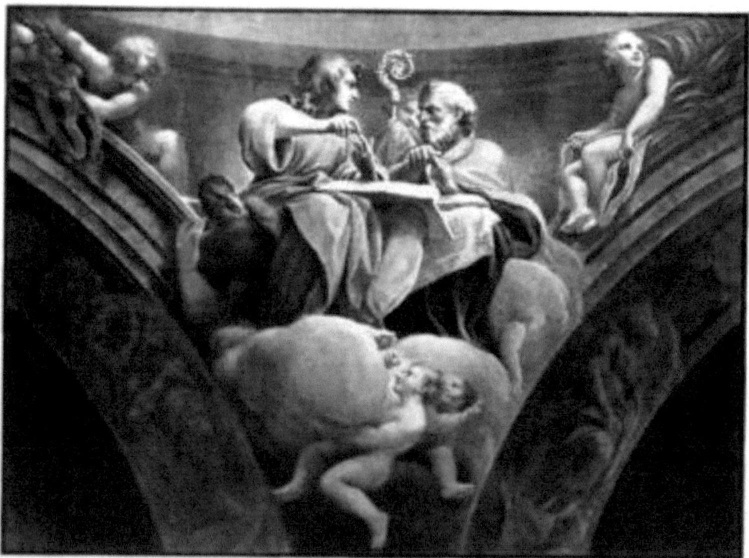

ST. JOHN AND ST. AUGUSTINE
Church of S. Giovanni Evangelista, Parma

Henceforth the life of Augustine was filled with Christian labors. After some ten years of devout living he became the bishop of Hippo (near Carthage) where he resided for thirty-five years, until his death in 430. All his stores of learning were devoted to the explanation of Christian theology. He wrote a great number of treatises refuting what he believed to be heresies, and setting forth what he considered the true doctrines of the faith. An old writer pronounced him "sweet in speech, wise in letters, and a noble worker in the labours of the church." In a book of "Confessions" he laid bare all his faults with great humility.

In our picture the good bishop is learning the truths of the faith from St. John, while a child-angel behind him holds his crosier and mitre. Allowing for the difference of ages, there is a certain resemblance between the two men, showing that they have in common a refined and sensitive nature, and an ardent temperament. The older man's face shows lines of thought and character. [42]

St. John seems to be counting off the points of the discussion on his fingers: it may be that he is unfolding the doctrine of the Trinity. The bishop follows the argument slowly, imitating St. John's gesture with hesitating hands. What seems so clear to the eager young teacher requires much deliberation on the part of the learner. The old man knits his brows with an intent expression, striving to understand the mystery. The two earnest faces turned towards each other make an interesting contrast.

The angel figures of the pendentive are worthy of notice. Three little creatures are frolicking on the clouds below the saints' feet, and two are perched on the upper part of the arches. They are wingless sprites, playful as human children, but with a grace and beauty not of earth. Two seem to be emerging from a hiding-place in the clouds, and gaily hail their comrade on the arch above. The lovely sprite on the opposite arch is thinking of other things, and looks over his shoulder across the church. The tiny fellow in charge of the mitre and crosier peeps out with a mischievous countenance.

Our reproduction shows a portion of the soffits, or under sides of the arches, decorated with figures from Old Testament history, painted in monochrome.

[43]

VIII

ST. MATTHEW AND ST. JEROME

The apostle Matthew was employed as a tax-gatherer in Jerusalem when he became a disciple of Jesus. He was sitting one day at the receipt of customs, when Jesus passed by and said unto him, "Follow me." "And he left all, rose up and followed him." [17] Soon after, the new disciple made a great feast for the Master, scandalizing the scribes and Pharisees by inviting guests of doubtful reputation. Matthew, however, had rightly judged the spirit of Jesus, who had come "not to call the righteous, but sinners to repentance." Throughout the ministry of Jesus, Matthew remained a faithful disciple, but without distinguishing himself in any way. Evidently he had a thoughtful mind and a good memory. In his Gospel he reported very fully the Sermon on the Mount and many of the parables.

[17] St. Luke, chapter v., verse 28.

One of the pendentives of the cupola in the church of S. Giovanni Evangelista is devoted to St. Matthew in company with St. Jerome. The Evangelist turns from the open Gospel before him to speak to St. Jerome, who is occupied with his writing. A winged cherub, sitting on a cloud in front of him, supports his book with both outstretched arms. [44] The cherub is St. Matthew's emblem, as the eagle is that of St. John. It is by this charming figure that the old masters represented the face of "a man," that is, the human face, in the "living creature" of Ezekiel's vision. [18] The symbol is appropriately applied to the first Evangelist because his Gospel emphasizes the humanity of Jesus.

[18] See also pages 34, 35.

The token of St. Jerome's identity is the cardinal's hat, held by an angel on the arch beside him. The two volumes on his lap, in addition to the scroll upon which he is engaged, show how busy has been the pen of this learned Father. As the old chronicler relates, "he never rested day ne night, but always read or wrote." [19]

[19] The life of St. Jerome is related in the *Golden Legend*. See Caxton's translation, in the *Temple Classics*, vol. v., page 199. Mrs. Jameson gives a condensed account of the same in *Sacred and Legendary Art*, page 280.

He came of a rich family, and received at Rome the best education afforded by his times. Like his contemporary, St. Augustine, he devoted all his scholarship to the service of the Christian faith. While St. Augustine's tastes were more philosophical, St. Jerome's were perhaps more for pure learning and the study of the classics. He made himself master of Hebrew and Greek, and his most valuable work was his translations. He rendered into Latin, which was the literary language of his day, the various books of the Old and New Testament, and this version became the authorized Bible or Vulgate.

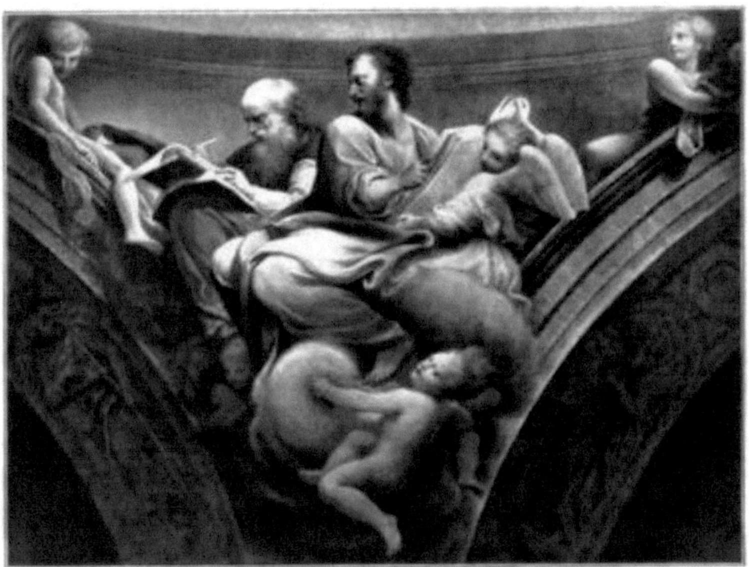

ST. MATTHEW AND ST. JEROME
Church of S. Giovanni Evangelista, Parma

Please click on the image for a larger image.

St. Jerome was a Dalmatian by birth, but in the [47] course of his life he journeyed to many countries. Soon after his baptism, he visited Syria, to retrace the scenes of the life of Christ. He then retired to a desert, where he passed four years in penance and fasting, living in the companionship of wild beasts. Clothed in sackcloth, he spent his days in torture, struggling with temptation, and haunted by visions of demons.

At a later period of his life he was in Rome, where he gained an immense influence over fashionable women. Two of his converts here were Paula and Marcella, whose names are historical. Finally he returned to Palestine, and passed the remainder of his days in a monastery which he had founded in Bethlehem. He was a man of vehement nature, a violent partisan, and an untiring student.

Something of his character may be seen in the face of the old man of our picture, bending over his writing. He seems so absorbed in his task that he is entirely unconscious of his surroundings. The deep-set eyes, overhung by shaggy brows, are fixed intently on his scroll. From his association with St. Matthew, we may fancy that he is translating the first Gospel. The Evangelist, with his own volume before him, is supervising the work. He turns to the translator with an encouraging smile, and seems to dictate the words. St. Matthew's face is gentle and amiable, though not so strong as we are wont to imagine it. He is here represented in middle life, at about the age when called to discipleship.

As in the pendentive of St. John and St. Augus [48] tine, the angel figures add an element of beauty to the picture. Each one seems attracted by some distant object. The cherub holding St. Matthew's book looks towards the worshippers in the church. Some one in the congregation also seems to attract the attention of the angel with the cardinal's hat, and he smiles shyly, as if in reply to a gesture of admiration. His companion on the other arch turns his eyes towards the figures in the dome, where the apostles are enthroned on clouds. The playful little fellow on the clouds below St. Matthew's feet looks across at the sprites of the opposite pendentive.

All this charming by-play gives the impression of a company of living spirits frolicking among the arches of the church. "Have Correggio's *putti* [20] grown up yet and walked out of their frames?" the painter, Guido Reni, used to ask, referring with quaint humor to the wonderful lifelikeness of such child figures. So, looking at these angels, we half expect to see them wave a hand to us over the arches, and, turning with a sudden motion, disappear from our sight among the clouds.

[20] Italian for "boys."

[49]

IX

THE REST ON THE RETURN FROM EGYPT

(The Madonna della Scodella)

Before the child Jesus was two years old, he was taken on a journey which at that time was long and tedious. An angel appeared to Joseph one night in a dream, saying, "Arise, and take the young child and his mother, and flee into Egypt, and be thou there until I bring thee word; for Herod will seek the young child to destroy him."

The news of Jesus' birth had been first brought to King Herod by the wise men of the East, who came in search of the new-born king whose star they had seen. The idea of a strange ruler to usurp the throne alarmed Herod, and he determined to be rid of any possible rival. Accordingly orders were given to slay all children in and near Bethlehem "from two years old and under."

While this terrible slaughter was going on, the Holy Family were making their way to the strange land of refuge. Here they lived, awaiting heavenly guidance for their return. "But when Herod was dead, behold an angel of the Lord appeareth in a dream to Joseph in Egypt, saying, Arise, and take the young child and his mother, and go into the land of Israel; for they are dead which sought [50] the young child's life. And he arose, and took the young child and his mother, and came into the land of Israel." [21]

[21] The quotations are from St. Matthew, chapter ii.

This is all the Evangelist tells us of what was doubtless an exciting, perhaps even a perilous adventure. We may suppose both journeys to have been made by donkeys, the common beasts of burden in Eastern countries. The young mother and child must certainly have had to ride. As for Joseph, he was a sturdy man, and may well have walked; in those days travelling was a matter of time. Unused to luxuries, these simple folk trusted in Providence to supply their few needs by the way.

Our picture illustrates an imaginary incident on the return journey from Egypt to Israel. It is the hour of the noonday rest, and the little company have come to a halt in the woods. An old legend relates how at such times the trees would bend to offer them fruit, and springs would gush forth out of the dry ground for their refreshment. Mary has seated herself on a bank by the stream, while Joseph plucks the fruit from the date palm near by.

The boy Jesus has been standing between the two, watching Joseph, from whose outstretched hand he now takes the fruit. At the same time he is thirsty, and leaning back towards his mother, he turns and throws an arm over her shoulder, asking for a drink of water. She has a round basin (or *scodella*) which the family use as a drinking-cup, and the child points to it with a coaxing smile, resting his hand on her wrist.

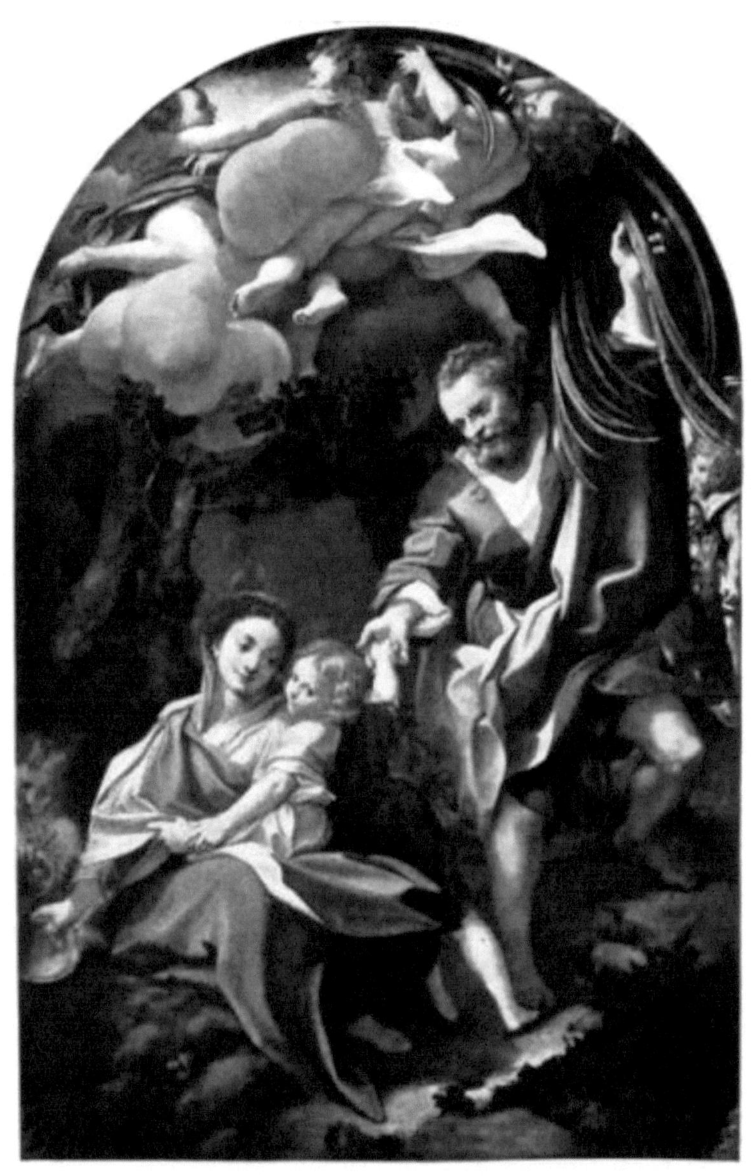

THE REST ON THE RETURN FROM EGYPT (MADONNA DELLA

SCODELLA)
Parma Gallery

Please click on the image for a larger image.

Please click here for a modern color image

[53]

Mary turns with fond pride towards the dear little face so near
her own. Her face is the same which we have already seen bending
in a mother's first ecstasy over her babe. Here it has a maturer and
more matronly look, but with no less sweetness. Joseph, from his
higher level, looks down kindly upon the two. His generous nature
seems to take delight in anything that gives them pleasure. He is
large and heavily built, a stalwart protector should perils beset
them. In spite of the thick draperies so clumsily wound about him,
he is a dignified figure. He holds here a place of prominence seldom
given him by other painters.

The child upon whom so much love is lavished is a tall, lithe boy
with a well shaped head. His hair is parted, and falls in loose curls
on each side of a forehead which marks him a child of genius. The
face is delicate and sensitive, with a shy expression in the eyes.

The family are not alone, for, all unseen by them, a company of
ministering angels wait upon them. A tall one in the rear takes care
of the donkey. Another little creature peeps from the thicket beside
Mary. Four more circle overhead among the branches of the trees,
borne upon little clouds which they have brought with them from
the upper regions. Their wind-blown hair and fluttering garments
show how swift is their motion. One of them tugs mightily at the
palm, throwing himself backward in the effort to bend it towards
Joseph. Two others sport together with interlocked arms, and higher still, a pair of [54] eyes gleam through the leaves. The whole joc-
und company seem to fill the place with mirth. They fulfil the prom-
ise of the ancient psalmist, "He shall give his angels charge over
thee, to keep thee in all thy ways."

Certain characteristics of Correggio's art are well illustrated in the
picture. His delight in the foot is here almost equal to that he shows
for the hand in "The Marriage of St. Catherine." The three wayfarers
travel with bare feet, and the ministering angels flaunt their feet

gaily in the air. Drawn in many positions, it is interesting to see how decorative this feature of the picture is.

The figures are cleverly grouped, that they may completely fill the tall, narrow panel. The composition is built on a diagonal plan. From the left hand of Joseph, grasping the palm branch, to the right hand of Mary, with the basin of water, runs the strong main line which gives character to the drawing. The child links the two larger figures together, by stretching out a hand to each. The group of cloud-borne angels above also follows a diagonal direction parallel to the larger group. We shall presently see that the painter used the same method of composition in another picture.

The opening beyond the copse, where the donkey is tied, makes the spot seem less gloomy and isolated. It is an important principle of art to represent no enclosed place without a glimpse of light in the background.

[55]

X

ECCE HOMO

The old Hebrew prophet who wrote of the coming Messiah predicted that he should be "despised and rejected of men, a man of sorrows, and acquainted with grief." How fully the prophecy was realized, we may read in the narrative of the trial and crucifixion of Jesus.

The enemies of Jesus had to deal with their prisoner according to the formality of the Roman law. They brought him to the Roman governor, Pontius Pilate, accusing him of "perverting the nation, and forbidding to give tribute to Cæsar, saying that he himself is Christ, a king." [22] The governor duly examined Jesus, but, finding no case against him, proposed to scourge him and let him go.

[22] St. Luke, chapter xxiii., verse 2.

"Then Pilate therefore took Jesus and scourged him. And the soldiers platted a crown of thorns and put it on his head, and they put on him a purple robe, and said, Hail, King of the Jews! and they smote him with their hands. Pilate therefore went forth again, and saith unto them, Behold, I bring him forth to you, that ye may know that I find no fault in him. [56]

"Then came Jesus forth, wearing the crown of thorns, and the purple robe. And Pilate saith unto them, Behold the man! When the chief priests therefore and officers saw him, they cried out, saying Crucify him, Crucify him." [23] Pilate again sought to release Jesus, but the people continued to clamor, "Away with him," "Crucify him." "Then delivered he him therefore unto them to be crucified." [24]

[23] St. John, chapter xix., verses 1-6.

[24] *Ib.*, verse 16.

The Latin form of Pilate's words, "Behold the man," has given the title "Ecce Homo" to our picture. It is the moment when Jesus comes forth from the rude mockery of the soldiers, clad in a royal robe, and wearing the crown of thorns. The governor has bidden one of the soldiers lead the prisoner out on a balcony of the palace. An eager throng of people are waiting outside, but they are not all enemies. Among them are a few faithful women, and they are allowed to press close to the balcony. At the sight of her son, treated as a criminal with bound hands, the mother, Mary, falls swooning over the balustrade, supported by a younger woman.

Pilate standing in the doorway behind appeals to the crowd: "I find no fault in him. Behold the man." He has been deeply impressed by his interview with Jesus, and is willing to do something in his behalf. His face is good-natured, we see, but with no strength of character in it. He is a handsome man with curling beard carefully trimmed, apparently not a hard man to deal with, but easy-going and selfish.

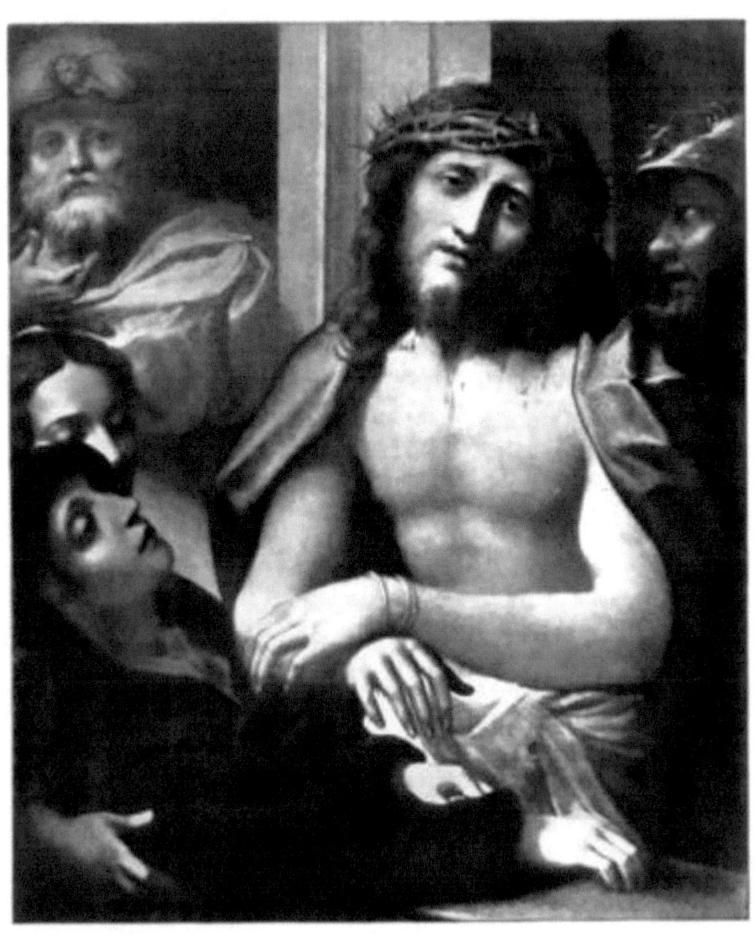

ECCE HOMO
National Gallery, London

Please click on the image for a larger image.

Please click here for a modern color image

[59]

Jesus stands with drooping head and an expression of suffering resignation. In the menacing faces before him he sees the hatred which will be satisfied with nothing less than his death. Already he hears the cruel cry, "Crucify him, crucify him." His badge of kingship is the crown of suffering. Were his kingdom of this world, his servants would deliver him from his enemies. As the ruler of a heavenly kingdom, he was born "to bear witness unto the truth."

The rich mantle, which the soldiers have mockingly thrown over his shoulders, falls away and shows the body as it had been bared for the scourging. It is a beautiful form, perfectly developed, and the arms and hands are as delicately modelled as a woman's. The face is oval, with regular features of classic mould, a short parted beard, and long hair falling in disordered curls about it. This is the typical face of Christ, as it has been handed down from generation to generation since early in the Christian era. The rude pictures in the catacombs are on the same model. So faithfully has the type been followed through the centuries, some believe that the original must have been an authentic likeness. [25]

[25] See *Rex Regum*, by Sir Wyke Bayliss.

The mother Mary is still young and beautiful. As the great Michelangelo said, "Purity enjoys eternal youth." [26] A heavy veil or mantle is draped [60] over her head, framing the pure profile of her face. This form of drapery is common among the old masters in painting Mary as *Mater Dolorosa,* or the Sorrowing Mother.

[26] See the volume on Michelangelo in the *Riverside Art Series*, page 35.

Artistically considered, this figure of the fainting mother is the finest thing in the picture. Her companion, probably Mary Magdalene, is also a lovely creature, though we see only a part of her face.

The subject is in tragic contrast to the illustrations we have just been studying. It seems strange to connect this Man of Sorrows with the happy boy we saw by the woodland spring, or this grief-stricken woman with that proud young mother. Correggio himself, we know, shrank from such sad themes.

Like the picture of The Marriage of St. Catherine, our illustration shows how skilfully Correggio painted hands. The drooping fingers of the Saviour taper delicately, with long almond-shaped nails. Pilate's hand has slender, flexible fingers like those of some dainty woman, and might be mated with that of Mary Magdalene. It is apparent that the study of hands and feet interested our painter more than that of faces. We shall lose much in his pictures if we do not give special attention to these features. In the case before us, the face of Christ must be less attractive, on account of the sorrowful expression. To make up, as it were, for this, the hands are brought into prominent notice, and are very beautiful.

[61]

XI

APOSTLES AND GENII

The glory of Parma is the Cathedral, which represents the labors of many centuries. The building itself was begun in 1058, and completed in the thirteenth century. The interior was beautified by a succession of artists, one of whom was our painter Correggio. His work here was the decoration of the cupola, and he began it immediately upon finishing the frescoes in the church of S. Giovanni Evangelista.

The Cathedral dome is octagonal in shape. In the roof, or topmost space, the Virgin Mary seems borne on circling throngs of saints and angels to meet the Saviour in the upper air. Below the dome runs a cornice, or frieze, in eight sections, filled with figures of apostles gazing upon the vision. Still lower are four decorated pendentives, similar to those in the church of S. Giovanni Evangelista. These contain respectively the four patron saints of Parma.

To the spectator looking up from below, the effect is of "a moving vision, rapturous and ecstatic." A multitude of radiant figures sweep and whirl through the heavenly spaces. "They are upon every side, bending, tossing, floating, and diving through the [62] clouds, hovering above the abysmal void that is between the dome and the earth below it." [27] Wonderful indeed is the triumph of the painter's art in this place. "Reverse the cupola and fill it with gold, and even that will not represent its worth," said Titian.

[27] E. H. Blashfield in *Italian Cities.*

Our illustration shows a portion of the octagonal cornice. The design is a simulated balcony ornamented with tall candelabra. In

front stand the apostles grouped in twos at the corners. On the top
of the balustrade, in the spaces between the candelabra, sport a
band of genii, or heavenly spirits.

The four apostles are men of giant frames with broad shoulders
and stalwart limbs. They are of middle age, heavily bearded, and all
look much alike. It would be impossible to call one Peter, and another Paul, or to identify any particular persons. Evidently it was
not the intention of the artist to distinguish individuals. All the
figures are turned with lifted faces towards the vision in the dome.
Each expresses, by a gesture, the wonder, joy, rapture, or admiration aroused by the spectacle. Their attitudes are somewhat extrav-
agant and self-conscious. The drapery, too, is rather fantastic, flung
about their figures, leaving arms and legs bare. Were the picture
taken out of its surroundings it would scarcely suggest a Christian
subject. These colossal beings are like Titans moving through the
figures of a sacred dance, and murmuring the mystic incantations of
some heathen rite.

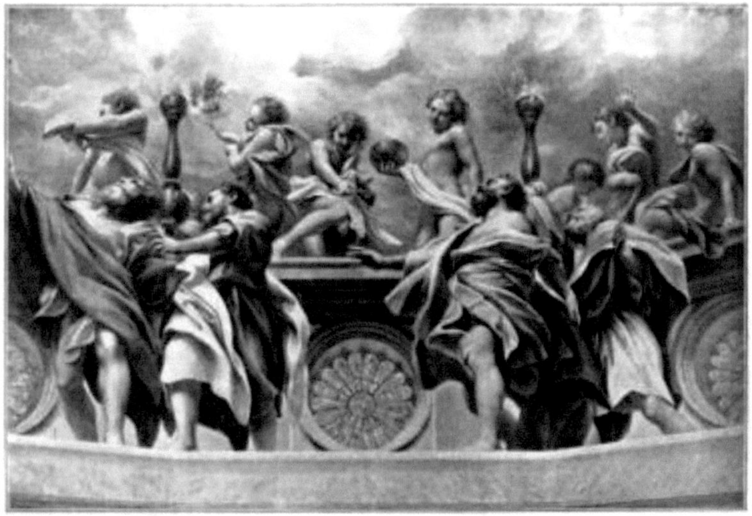

APOSTLES AND GENII
Cathedral, Parma

Please click on the image for a larger image.

[65]

But we must not press our interpretation too far. The panel should be studied for its decorative quality as a part of a larger scheme. Viewed from below, this procession of figures must be exceedingly effective. The emphasis of lines is diagonal, flowing in the direction of the focal point of the whole decoration.

The genii of the balustrade are beings of Correggio's own creation. His imagination called forth a world of spirits without a counterpart in the work of any other painter. Lacking the wings usually given in art to angels, they also lack the proper air of sanctity for heavenly habitants. Yet they are far too ethereal for mortals. Neither angel nor human, they are rather sprites of elf-land. With their tossing hair and agile motions they remind us of woodland creatures, and they look shyly out of their eyes like the furtive folk of the forest.

They are sportive, but not mischievous, in the human sense. They frolic in the pure delight of motion. By mortal standards of age they are between childhood and youth, when limbs are long and bodies supple. Their only draperies are narrow scarfs which they twist about them in every conceivable way.

Of the seven figures seen in our illustration, two only have any ostensible purpose to serve. One seems to be lighting a candelabrum with a flambeau; another carries a bowl which may be used for incense. The others are idlers. If they have any duties as acolytes, these are for the moment for [66] gotten. Several are attracted by the ceremonies in the cathedral and look down from their high perch upon the worshipping congregation.

The sprite at the extreme right is seated, and peeps over his shoulder with a rather dreamy expression. Next come two who are playing together, one throwing up his left arm as if to balance himself. Beyond the candelabrum is one whose parted hair and coquettish pose of the head give a feminine look to the figure. The sprite in the centre of the balustrade is the most winsome of the company. His bright eyes have spied out some one in the congregation, and stooping, he points directly at the person. His expression is very roguish. The little fellow with the flambeau is at the left, and last is one whose face is turned away towards the imaginary space behind the balcony.

Our illustration gives us a general idea of Correggio's decorative method. The human body was his material; his patterns were woven of nude figures, posed in every possible attitude. Every figure is in motion, and the whole multitude palpitates with the joy of living.

[67]

XII

ST. JOHN THE BAPTIST

In one of the pendentives of the cupola in the Parma Cathedral is the figure of St. John the Baptist reproduced in our illustration. The background is made to resemble somewhat the interior of a shell. On billows of clouds sits the prophet, with a lamb in his arms, and a circle of angels playing about him.

St. John the Baptist was a cousin of Jesus, and the first to recognize the true character of the carpenter's son. While Jesus was still living in obscurity in Nazareth, John went forth to preach in the wilderness about the river Jordan. His manner of life was very singular. He "had his raiment of camel's hair and a leathern girdle about his loins; and his meat was locusts and wild honey." [28]

[28] St. Matthew, chapter iii., verse 4.

The preacher was stern in denouncing sin and in warning evil-doers of the wrath to come. The burden of all his sermons was, "Repent, for the kingdom of heaven is at hand." When the people asked him what they ought to do, his answers were full of common sense. "He that hath two coats, let him impart to him that hath none; and he that hath meat, let him do likewise." To the tax-collectors, [68] he said, "Exact no more than that which is appointed you;" to the soldiers, "Do violence to no man, neither accuse any falsely." [29]

[29] St. Luke, chapter iii.

The authorities sent from Jerusalem to question the claims of the strange preacher; but his reply was in the words of the old Hebrew prophet, "I am the voice of one crying in the wilderness." [30]

[30] St. John, chapter i., verse 23.

It was the custom of John to baptize his converts in the river Jordan. One day Jesus presented himself for baptism, and John saw in him one whose shoe's latchet he was not worthy to unloose. At once he proclaimed him to the people as the "Lamb of God who taketh away the sins of the world." [31]

[31] *Ib.*, verse 29.

With the entrance of Jesus upon his ministry, John's work was fulfilled. "He must increase, but I must decrease," said the prophet humbly. [32] He was soon after cast into prison by King Herod, whose vices he had openly rebuked. Thence he was taken out only to be executed.

[32] St. John, chapter iii., verse 30.

It must be confessed that Correggio cared very little about making a true character study of St. John. There is not much in the figure of our pendentive to suggest the stern and fearless prophet of the wilderness. The humility of the countenance is perhaps the feature most appropriate to the character. The shy, haunting expression in the eyes is, too, such as belongs to one who, like St. John, lived much alone in the woods. The tunic is short and sleeveless, showing the strong limbs of the hermit.

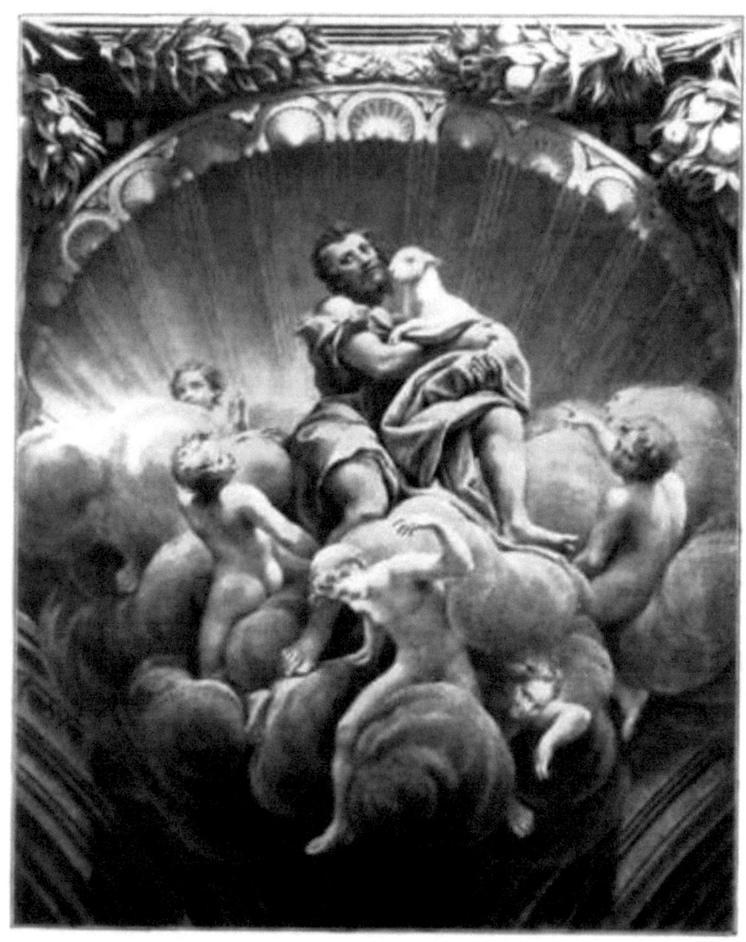

ST. JOHN THE BAPTIST
Cathedral, Parma

Please click on the image for a larger image.

[71]

For the rest, the Baptist's face has the same gentle amiability we
have already seen in St. Matthew and Joseph. The type is a common
one with Correggio. A certain resemblance runs through nearly all

his male figures, whether of smooth-faced youth, bearded manhood, or hoary old age.

The tenderness of St. John for his little lamb is the chief motive of the picture. He carries it on his left arm, supporting the weight on his knee, and the innocent creature puts its nose close to the prophet's face. The lamb is the accepted symbol of St. John the Baptist, in allusion to the words with which he addressed Jesus at the Jordan, "Behold the lamb of God." The same figure is used in the book of Revelation, where the Lamb is described "in the midst of the throne." Standing for the person of Christ himself, St. John holds the sacred emblem with reverence. To understand why his face is lifted in this direction we must remember that his glance is directed toward the vision in the dome just above.

The angel figures of this pendentive are among the most beautiful and characteristic of the myriad throng of the cupola. The impression made by this great spirit company upon one standing beneath the dome has been described in some lines by Aubrey de Vere:—

> "Creatures all eyes and brows and tresses streaming,
> By speed divine blown back; within all fire
> Of wondering zeal, and storm of bright desire.
> Round the broad dome the immortal throngs are beaming,
> With elemental powers the vault is teeming;
> We gaze, and gazing join the fervid choir,
> In spirit launched on wings that ne'er can tire."
> [72]

While the spirits in the upper part of the cupola are massed so closely together that we do not see the full beauty of each one, these in our picture may be studied separately. There are six in all, and their purpose is to call the attention of the worshippers to the prophet. The two in the rear, whose bodies are hidden in the clouds, gaze upon him adoringly. One on each side points with outstretched finger to the lamb, as if repeating the Baptist's words, "Behold the lamb of God." The angel astride the cloud in front was interrupted in the same task by a little fellow suddenly shooting out from the clouds beneath him. He peers into the opening at one side, but still lifts his left hand towards the prophet above him.

The six figures are arranged in a semicircle, and their slender limbs and lithe bodies trace rhythmic lines of grace. The most charming of the company is perhaps he at the right, whose eyes meet ours with a bewitching smile.

[73]

XIII

CHRIST APPEARING TO MARY MAGDALENE IN THE GARDEN

(Noli me tangere)

It was Sunday, the third day after the crucifixion of Jesus. Early in the morning, while it was yet dark, a young woman made her way to the rock-hewn tomb in the garden of Joseph of Arimathea. It was Mary Magdalene, whom Jesus had rescued from a life of sin. Much had been forgiven her, therefore she loved much. In her sorrow she came to visit the spot where the body of her crucified Master had been laid.

Great was her surprise to find that the stone placed at the entrance of the tomb had been rolled away. In her perplexity, she ran to tell the disciples Peter and John. They all hurried back together to the garden, and the two men, entering the tomb, found it empty. Unable to explain the mystery, they presently returned home, leaving Mary still standing without the sepulchre weeping.

"And as she wept, she stooped down, and looked into the sepulchre, and seeth two angels in white sitting, the one at the head, and the other at the feet, where the body of Jesus had lain. And they [74] say unto her, Woman, why weepest thou? She saith unto them, Because they have taken away my Lord, and I know not where they have laid him.

"And when she had thus said, she turned herself back, and saw Jesus standing, and knew not that it was Jesus. Jesus saith unto her, Woman, why weepest thou? whom seekest thou? She, supposing him to be the gardener, saith unto him, Sir, if thou have borne him hence, tell me where thou hast laid him, and I will take him away. Jesus saith unto her, Mary. She turned herself, and saith unto him, Rabboni; which is to say, Master.

"Jesus saith unto her, Touch me not; for I am not yet ascended to my Father: but go to my brethren, and say unto them, I ascend unto my Father, and your Father; and to my God, and your God." [33]

[33] Chapter xx. of the Gospel according to St. John, verses 11-17.

Our picture illustrates the story of that first Easter morning. Jesus has greeted Mary by name, and she has instantly recognized the Master. Sinking on her knees, she would have impulsively stretched out her hands to him, but he repels her with a gesture. Awe-struck, she gazes into his face, while he explains the message she is to carry to the disciples.

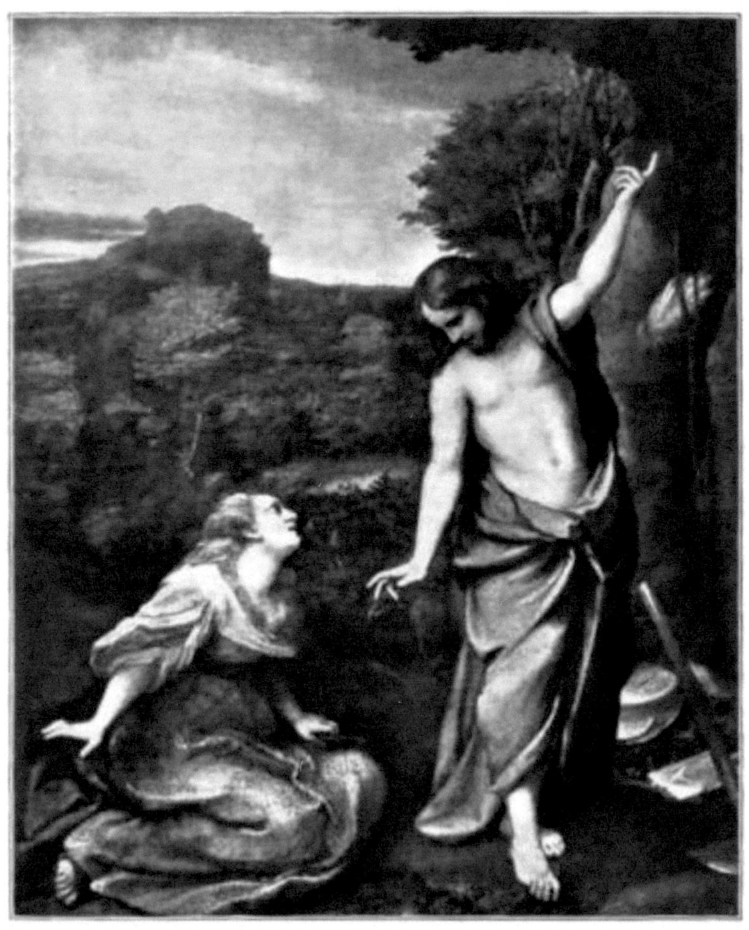

CHRIST APPEARING TO MARY MAGDALENE IN THE GARDEN
(NOLI ME TANGERE)
Prado Gallery, Madrid

Please click on the image for a larger image.

Please click here for a modern color image

The risen Lord is clad in but one garment, a heavy mantle, knot-ted at the waist. The upper part is slipping from his shoulders, leav-ing the torso bare. The beauty of the form reminds us of a Greek

68

statue. On the ground beside him are some garden tools, a [77] hoe and a spade, and beyond these lies a straw hat. These things explain why Mary, blinded and confused with weeping, supposed that it was the gardener who spoke to her.

The Master's attitude and gesture emphasize the meaning of his words. The body sways slightly to one side, as if shrinking from Mary's touch. He still holds his right hand outstretched, as when he said "Touch me not." And now he raises his left arm, and pointing heavenward declares that he is about to ascend to his Father. He seems to speak gently as to a child, and looks down into Mary's face with a smile.

The young woman is richly arrayed in a brocade dress, cut so as to show her beautiful neck and arms. A mass of wavy golden hair falls over her shoulders and upon her bosom. Her tapering wrists and delicate hands indicate gentle blood, but her features are somewhat heavy, and the face would not attract us by its beauty. The rapt expression of devotion is what makes it interesting. The whole attitude expresses complete self-forgetfulness.

The lithe and youthful figure of Christ recalls the boy we saw in a former picture journeying from Egypt. We can see that this is the man into whom that child is grown. We note again the high full forehead over which the parted hair is brushed in curves. Again, too, we see the small mouth with the gentle smile. The figure in general features resembles the Christ type which is illustrated in the picture of Ecce Homo. [78]

In painting the figure of the risen Christ, the old masters were accustomed to give prominence to the nail prints in hands and feet, and the wound in his side. Correggio has not done this. Such signs of suffering were inconsistent with the joyous nature of his art. The subject of the picture is entirely a happy one, and he has kept out of it all evidences of the crucifixion, emphasizing rather the idea of the ascension.

In some artistic points our picture resembles the Madonna della Scodella. The pose of Christ is similar to that of Joseph, with one arm lifted up, and the other reaching down. Thus is formed the diagonal line which is at the basis of the composition. The right arm of Mary carries the line on to the lower corner of the picture.

The landscape setting makes a spacious background, and a large tree behind Christ throws his figure into relief.

[79]

XIV

THE MADONNA OF ST. JEROME

(Il Giorno)

It is a bright clear day, and a baby boy is having a rare frolic out of doors, on his mother's knee. It is the little Christ-child, and his visitors are St. Jerome and Mary Magdalene. Overhead a red cloth drapery has been stretched from tree to tree, making a sort of canopy to protect the company from the direct rays of the sun. St. Jerome has brought as an offering the books which represent the scholarly toil of many years. Mary Magdalene has her jar of ointment for the anointing of the Saviour's feet.

The mother sits on a slight elevation in the centre, her bare foot resting on the ground. St. Jerome stands in front, a little at one side, where he can hold a book directly before the child's face. Mary Magdalene, half kneeling on the other side, stoops to caress a little foot. The sturdy old father seems to have come directly from his monastery in Bethlehem, and his lion follows him like a faithful dog. The old legend relates that as he sat one evening at his monastery gate, a lion approached, holding up a paw which was pierced with a thorn. The good [80] father removed the thorn and dressed the wound, and the grateful beast became thenceforth the constant companion of his benefactor.

The scroll in St. Jerome's right hand may be any one of his many treatises or translations. The large open volume is undoubtedly his Latin version of the Bible. One side of the book is supported on his left hand, while the other is held by an attendant angel, who turns the pages for the Christ-child. There is something very interesting on the page now open, and the angel points a slender finger to a particular passage. The child is wrought up to the highest pitch of

70

excitement. He stretches out his legs and arms, his whole body stiffening in a tremor of joy. He fairly pants with eagerness for the treasure just beyond his grasp. Though not a pretty boy, he is so full of life that we find him very captivating.

Old St. Jerome looks immensely pleased with the child's delight. The angel playfellow is delighted with his success in amusing the baby, and laughs sympathetically with him. The mother smiles with gentle indulgence, and holds him firmly lest he spring from her arms. Mary Magdalene appears almost unconscious of what is going on. Her whole being is absorbed in loving devotion. She has caught one little foot lightly by the heel, and, drawing it towards her, lays her cheek against the soft knee. Her hair is unbound, and falls in long tresses over her neck. In throwing out his arms, the child's left hand has fallen on the golden head, and here it rests as if he returned the caress. In the mean time a mischievous [83] urchin, who may be the boy Baptist, holds the Magdalene's jar of ointment. He stands behind her like a small lackey, and sniffs curiously at the contents of the pot.

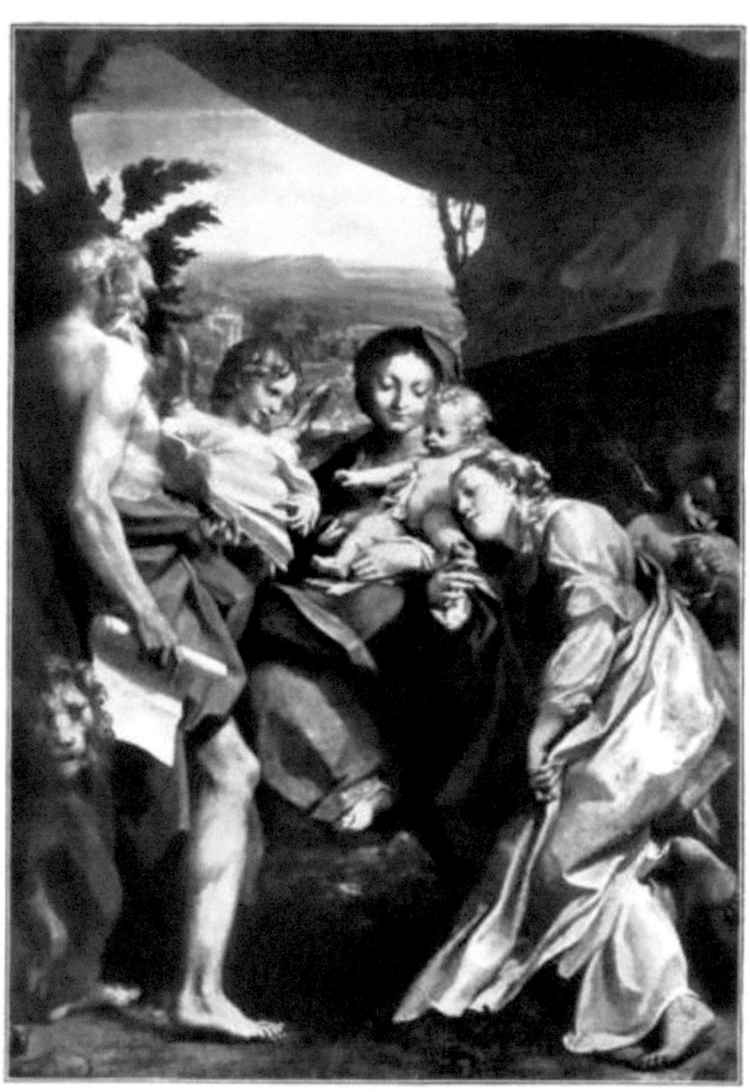

THE MADONNA OF ST. JEROME
Parma Gallery

Please click on the image for a larger image.

Please click here for a modern color image

If it seems strange that St. Jerome and Mary Magdalene should be here together, we must remember that the painters of Correggio's time did not try to represent sacred scenes with historical accuracy. It was customary to bring together in a picture persons who lived in altogether different periods and countries. The meaning of such pictures was symbolic. The Christians of all ages constitute a communion of the saints who meet at the Christ-child's feet.

The two saints here make a fine artistic contrast, — the rugged and grizzled old man, and the lovely golden-haired maiden. The splendid muscular strength of the one is offset against the radiant beauty of the other. In a devotional sense also the contrast is most appropriate. St. Jerome has served the Christ with great powers of intellect; Mary Magdalene brings only a woman's loving heart. The one has written great books; the other could do nothing but anoint the Saviour's feet. Yet the two kinds of service are equally important. St. Jerome's translations have carried the gospel over the world, and it is written that "Wheresoever this gospel shall be preached in the whole world, there shall also this, that this woman hath done, be told for a memorial of her." [34]

[34] St. Matthew, chapter xxvi., verse 13.

The composition of the picture is on a diagonal [84] plan similar to that which we have already noticed in his pictures. [35] The structural line may be traced from the top of St. Jerome's head across the shoulders and back of Mary Magdalene. The edge of the canopy overhead emphasizes this line by following the same general direction. The child's figure behind the Magdalene balances the figure of the lion in the left corner.

[35] See chapters IX. and XIII.

The landscape which lies beyond the canopy is an important and beautiful part of the picture. Without this spacious distance in the background the large figures filling the foreground would crowd the composition unpleasantly. It is a relief to the eye to traverse this stretch of sunny country.

The picture makes it possible for us to understand why Correggio has been called a painter of "light and space and motion." All three characteristics are admirably illustrated here. In color, too, the original painting is very fine. The Virgin wears the usual red robe and blue mantle, the colors denoting love and constancy. St. Jerome has a blue drapery about the hips and a crimson mantle, while the angel's tunic and Mary Magdalene's mantle are yellow.

It is the clear golden atmosphere flooding the scene which gives it the Italian name of "Il Giorno," The Day.

[85]

XV

CUPID SHARPENING HIS ARROWS

(Detail of Danaë)

In the imagination of the ancient Greeks all human love was inspired by the goddess Aphrodite, Venus, aided by her son, the little archer Cupid. It was Cupid's office to shoot the arrows of affection. Being a mischievous fellow, he took delight in aiming his shafts at the unsuspecting. Often his victims were so oddly chosen that it seemed as if the marksman had shot at random. Some believed that he did his work blindfolded.

The poets describe Cupid as a beautiful winged boy carrying a bow and a quiver of arrows, and sometimes a torch. He flew at will through the wide universe, but he loved best the island of Cyprus, which was his mother's first home. "His head has goodly curls," wrote Moschus, [36] "but impudent is the face he wears; his little hands are tiny, 'tis true, yet they shoot far.... Small is his arrow, yet it carries even to the sky.... He is naked indeed, so far as his body is concerned, but his mind is shrouded. And being winged as a bird he flies upon now one party of men and women and now another, and settles on their inmost hearts."

[36] In the first idyl, translated by J. Bank. [86]

74

The mingled pain and delight caused by a wound of love is explained by the fact that Cupid's arrows were tipped with gall and honey. The way in which they were fashioned is variously described by the poets. Anacreon has it that they were made at the forge of Vulcan, the husband of Venus, and the blacksmith of the gods. One of this poet's odes relates how —

> "In the Lemnian caves of fire
> The mate of her who nursed Desire
> Moulded the glowing steel to form
> Arrows for Cupid thrilling warm;
> While Venus every barb imbues
> With droppings of her honeyed dews;
> And Love (alas the victim heart)
> Tinges with gall the burning dart." [37]

[37] In Moore's translation.

A slightly different explanation is given by the Latin poet Claudian: —

> "In Cyprus' isle two rippling fountains fall
> And one with honey flows, and one with gall;
> In these, if we may take the tale from fame,
> The son of Venus dips his darts of flame."

However the story may run, there is but one ending. The victim of the love-god's arrow confesses that "loving is a painful thrill," but "not to love, more painful still."

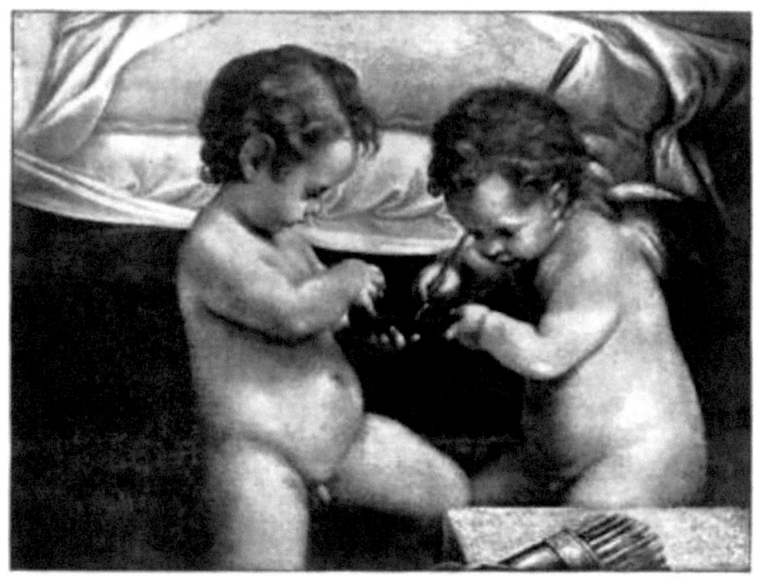

CUPID SHARPENING HIS ARROWS (DETAIL OF DANAË)
Borghese Gallery, Rome

Please click on the image for a larger image.

Please click here for a modern color image

So bold was the little archer that the mightiest could not withstand his arts. The war-god Mars, bringing his spear one day to Vulcan's forge, smiled contemptuously at the light shafts of Cupid. "Try it," said little Love, handing him one. Whereupon the foolish fellow cried out in an agony of pain, and [89] begged Cupid to take the arrow back. Apollo, the archer of the sun, was equally imprudent, and was richly punished for his sneers. An arrow from the fatal quiver made him mad with unrequited love for the nymph Daphne. A being who could give so much pain and pleasure was at once to be loved and feared. Hence all paid homage —

> "To Love, for heaven and earth adore him
> And gods and mortals bow before him."

In our picture, Cupid looks just as the poets have described him, a beautiful baby boy with wings and "goodly curls." Only the milk and honey of Cyprus could have made the little body so plump. A deep crease marks the line of his wrist, a soft fold of flesh the neck. The full quiver lies on the table beside him, and he is sharpening one of the darts. [38] A little companion helps him hold the whetstone steady while he presses the arrow tip upon its surface. Some lines of Horace come to mind describing —

> "Cupid sharpening all his fiery darts
> Upon a whetstone stained with blood of hearts."

[38] Vasari says that Cupid is trying the arrow on a stone.

Cupid's companion is as like him as a twin, save that he has no wings. He may be a human playfellow of the little god, or one of the brood of loves with which the poets have peopled Cyprus. While the original myth told of only one Cupid, imagination has multiplied his kind. We read of the "playful rout of Cupids" attendant upon the love-god, who rules as sovereign among them. [90]

The two children of the picture are intent upon their task. The very seriousness of their manner argues some mischief in view. Evidently they are preparing for a great conquest. The arrow must not fail of its work, but must be sharp enough to carry the sweet poison straight to the victim's heart.

Both of the chubby fellows have rather large heads with clustering ringlets. The wingless boy has the high, full forehead which marks an active mind. Cupid seems to have the more energetic temperament of the two, while his comrade is a bit of a dreamer.

Our picture is a charming illustration of Correggio's love of children. As it was not the fashion of his time to paint children's portraits, he had to make his own opportunities for the favorite subject. How ingenious he was we have had occasion to see in our study. When given a sacred subject to paint he filled all the available spaces with child angels sporting in the clouds. With the ceiling of a room to decorate, he covered the whole surface with a band of little boys at play.

Our reproduction is a detail of a larger picture illustrating the myth of Danaë. The two little figures are in the lower right corner of the canvas.

[91]

XVI

A SUPPOSED PORTRAIT OF CORREGGIO

Almost every celebrated painter has at some time in his life sat for his portrait. Many have painted their own likenesses, not so much from motives of vanity, but as a matter of artistic interest. Others have posed as models to their fellow painters.

Correggio was an exception in this regard. The old biographer Vasari made many efforts to procure a portrait, and concluded that "he never took it himself, nor ever had it taken by others, seeing that he lived much in retirement."

Our painter, as we have seen, was not a student of the face. Form and expression did not greatly interest him. He busied himself chiefly with problems of light and shade. This is perhaps the reason why he never thought it worth while to paint his portrait. He was not a traveller, and probably never visited any of the great art centres of his time. So he made no friends among the contemporary painters who would have been likely to make his portrait. In any case his busy life left little time for any work for himself, and if he thought at all of a portrait, he doubtless postponed it to some more convenient season. Waiting for such a time, his career was brought suddenly to an end. He died of fever in Correggio at the age of forty. [92]

In the passing centuries one picture after another has been put forward as a pretended portrait of Correggio. The painter's admirers were always eager to believe that a real likeness had at last been discovered. Though we cannot rely upon the genuineness of any of these, some are very interesting.

Such an one is our frontispiece, from a painting in the Parma Gallery, pointed out as Correggio's portrait. Whoever the original may have been, the expression is certainly animated and intelligent.

There is much humor and kindliness in the face. The unknown artist should have the credit for the gift of revealing the individual
character of his sitter.

Lacking an authentic portrait of the man Correggio, we have to
content ourselves with the short account of his character given by
Vasari. "He was a person," writes the biographer, "who held himself
in but slight esteem, nor could he ever persuade himself that he
knew anything satisfactorily respecting his art; perceiving its diffi-
culties, he could not give himself credit for approaching the perfection to which he would so fain have seen it carried; he was a man
who contented himself with very little, and always lived in the
manner of a good Christian."

[93]

PRONOUNCING VOCABULARY OF PROPER NAMES AND FOREIGN WORDS

EXPLANATION OF DIACRITICAL MARKS.

A Dash (¯) above the vowel denotes the long sound, as in fāte, ēve, tīme, nōte, ūse.

A Dash and a Dot (-) above the vowel denote the same sound, less prolonged.

A Curve (˘) above the vowel denotes the short sound, as in ădd, ĕnd, ĭll, ŏdd, ŭp.

A Dot (˙) above the vowel a denotes the obscure sound of a in pȧst, ȧbāte, Amĕricȧ.

A Double Dot (¨) above the vowel a denotes the broad sound of a in fäther, älms.

A Double Dot (..) below the vowel a denotes the sound of a in ba̤ll.

A Wave (~) above the vowel e denotes the sound of e in hẽr.

A Circumflex Accent (^) above the vowel o denotes the sound of o in bôrn.

A dot (.) below the vowel u denotes the sound of u in the French language.

n indicates that the preceding vowel has the French nasal tone.

g and k denote the guttural sound of ch in the German language.

th denotes the sound of th in the, this.

ç sounds like s.

c̠ sounds like k.

s̠ sounds like z.

g̅ is hard as in g̅et.

ġ is soft as in ġem.

- Allegri (äl-lā'grē).

- Altius cæteris Dei patefecit arcana (äl'tē̆-o͝os kī'tā-rē̆s dā'ē pä-tā-fā'-kĭt är-kä'nä).
- Ambrose (ăm'brōz).
- Anacreon (ăn-ăk'rē̆-ŏn).
- Antonio (än-tō'nē-ō).
- Apollo (à-pŏl´lō).
- Aphrodite (ăf-rṓ-dī'tē).
- Artemis (är'tē-mĭs).
- Arimathea (Ăr-ĭ-mà-thē´à).
- Athena (ă-thē'nà).
- Augustine (a̤'gŭs-tēn).
- Aurora (a̤-rō'rà).
- Austin (a̤s'tĭn).

- Bayliss, Wyke (wĭk bā'lĭs).
- Bethlehem (Bĕth'lēhĕm).
- Berenson (bā'rĕn-sŏn).
- Blashfield (blăsh'fēld).
- Burckhardt (b o͞o rk'härt).

- Cæsar (sē'zàr).
- candelabrum (kăn-dḗ-lā'brŭm).
- Carthage (kär'thāj).
- Catherine (kăth'ĕr-ĭn).
- Caxton (kăks'tŭn).
- Cavaliere (kä-vä-lē-ā'ra̤).
- chiaroscuro (kyä-rṓ-sk o͞o 'rṓ).
- Cicerone (chē-chā-rō'na̤).
- Claudian (cla̤'dĭ-a̤n).
- Correggio (kŏr-rĕd'jō).
- Costus (kŏs'tŭs).
- Comus (kō'mŭs).
- Cupid (Cū'pĭd).
- Cyprus (sī'prŭs).

- Dalmatian (dăl-mā'shản).
- Danaë (dā'nā̆-ē).
- Daphne (dăf'nē).
- Diana (dī-ăn'ả *or* dī-ā'nả).

- Ecce Homo (ĕk'kĕ *or* ĕk'sḗ hō'mō). [94]
- Egypt (ē'jĭpt).
- Endymion (ĕn-dĭm'ĭ-ŭn).
- Ephesus (ĕf'ḗ-sŭs).
- Ezekiel (ē-zē'kĭ-ĕl).

- Galilee (găl'ĭ̆-lē).
- Giorno, Il (ēl jôr'nō).
- Giovanni Evangelista (jō-vän'nē ā-vän-jā-lēs'tä).
- Guido Reni (gwē'dō rā'nē).

- Hazlitt (Hăz'lĭtt).
- Heilige Nacht (hī'lḗg-ŭ näkt).
- Heaton (hē'tŭn).
- Herod (Hĕr'ŏd).
- Hesperus (Hĕs'pẽrŭs).
- Hippo (Hĭp'pō).
- Horace (hôr'ā̆s).

- Ignem gladio ne fodias (ḗg'nĕm glä'-dḗ-ō nā fō'dḗ-äs).
- Israel (ĭz'rā-ĕl).

- Jameson (jā'mĕ-sŭn).
- Jerome (jē̄-rōm' *or* jĕr'ŏm).
- Jerusalem (Jĕrū'saĭ̃ĕm).
- Jordan (Jôr'dản).
- Judæa (jū-dē'a).

- Keats (kēts).
- Kugler (kōōg'lẽr).

- Layard (Lāy'ȧrd).
- Lemnian (Lĕm'nĭȧn).

- Madonna (Mȧdŏn'nȧ).
- Magdalene (Măg'dā-lēn).
- Marcella (mär-sĕl'ȧ).
- Matthew (mă'thū).
- Mater Dolorosa (mā'tĕr dŏl-ố-rō'sȧ *or* mä'tär dō-lō-rō'sä).
- Maxentius (măks-ĕn'shĭ-ŭs).
- Mars (Märs).
- Meyer (mī'ẽr).
- Michelangelo (mē-kĕl-än'jā-lō).
- Milan (mĭl'ȧn *or* mĭ-lăn').
- Monica (Mŏn'ĭcȧ).
- Moore (mōr *or* m o͞o r).
- Moschus (mŏs'kŭs).
- Morelli (mō-rĕl'ḗ).

- Nazareth (Năz'ȧrĕth).
- Nicodemus (nĭk-ō-dē'mŭs).
- Noli me tangere (nō'lḗ mā tän'gā-rȧ̇ *or* nō'lī mē tăn'jĕ-rḗ).
- Notte, La (lä nōt'tā).
- Numidia (Nūmĭd'ĭȧ).

- Palestine (Păl'ĕstīne).
- Paolo (Pä'ōlō).
- Parma (Pär'mä).
- Patmos (Păt'mŏs).
- Paula (pa̤'lä).
- Pharisee (făr'ĭ-sē).
- Piacenza (pē-ä-chĕn'dzä).
- Plato (Plā'tō).
- Pontius Pilate (pŏn'shĭ-ŭs pĭ'lāt).
- putti (p o͞o t'tē).

- Rabboni (Răbbō'nĭ).
- Raphael (rä'fā-ĕl).

- Rex Regum (rāks rā'g $\overline{oo}$ m).
- Ricci, Corrado (kōr-rä'dō rēt'chē).
- Ruskin (Rŭs'kĭn).

- Sala del Pergolato (sä'lä dĕl pair-gō-lä'tō).
- Scipione Montino (shē-pē-ō'na᷼ mōn-tē'nō).
- Scodella (skō-dĕl'lä).
- Sebastian (sé-băst'yȧn).
- Simmonds (sĭm'ŭndz).
- Symonds (sĭm'ŭndz).
- Syria (sĭr'ĭ-ȧ).

- Te Deum (tā dā'$\breve{oo}$m *or* tē dē'ŭm).
- Titan (tī'tȧn).
- Titian (tĭsh'ȧn).

- Umbrian (ŭm'brĭ-ȧn).

- Vasari (vä-sä'rē̂).
- Venus (Vē'nŭs).
- Vere, Aubrey de (aa̤'brĭ dē vēr).
- Vulcan (Vŭl'cȧn).
- Vulgate (Vŭl'gāte).

- Wordsworth (wĕrdz'wĕrth).

- Zebedee (Zĕb'ĕdēē).